THE OTTAWA SCHOLAR

VOLUME THREE
2022
EDITED BY
JUSTIN CLARKE, PH.D.

urbanpress

The Ottawa Scholar-Volume Three, 2022
Edited by Justin Clarke, Ph.D.
Copyright ©2022 Ottawa University

ISBN 978-1-63360-192-5

For Worldwide Distribution
Printed in the U.S.A.

Urban Press
P.O. Box 8881
Pittsburgh, PA 15221-0881
412.646.2780
www.urbanpress.us

TABLE OF CONTENTS

PREFACE   v
FOREWORD   vii

SECTION ONE   FAITH BEIKMAN   2
                     ZOE BUTTS   5
                     JACKSON DAHM   9
                     BRENNA DILLER   12
                     ISAIAH EPP   15
                     CLEO FELTNER   18
                     RYLEE FIGGS   21
                     MACY GREUTER   24
                     NICHOLAS HATFIELD   27
                     MACEY MORRIS   31
                     EZEKIEL REAZIN   34
                     ANGELO REYES   37
                     BAYLER RINDLISBACHER   40
                     ELLISE ROMINE   42
                     LINDI SCHMELZER   47
                     ALEXIS SCHULTZE   50
                     KAYLA SMOCKS   53
                     MEADOW STULL   56
                     JULIA WALTMAN   59
                     DARBY WEIDL   62
                     ADDISON ZURCHER   66

SECTION TWO   HANNAH DEWARE   70
                     KARLEY FAUDERE   74
                     JONATHAN FOX   78
                     YAN KEUWO   82
                     DERRIANE MORRISON   86
                     ELI OWINGS   90

SECTION THREE   KAYLEN ASHLEY   96
                     BRODY BURKHOLDER   101
                     JESSAMINE GREUTER   106
                     COLLIN HANSON   110
                     LAWSON MEDLEN   116

SECTION FOUR   ANGEL GARRETT   122
                     BRYNDEN GROW   127

CONCLUSION   135

PREFACE

The third volume of *The Ottawa Scholar* is finished, and you are now holding it in your hands. It occurs to me that this is also our third year of living with COVID-19, and in each of the previous introductions, I optimistically noted my hope that we were near the end of the pandemic. I'm no longer willing to jinx it and make any predictions. I continue to be thankful to the administration at Ottawa University for making brave choices and committing to keep OU as open as possible and also for recognizing that in-person learning is extremely important for our students and faculty.

I hope that our scholars will find this volume valuable throughout their lives. Young scholars in their early academic career can use this book as an opportunity to look ahead at what their older counterparts are completing and preparing for — graduation and beyond. Older students can look back and reflect on all they have accomplished at OU. Then, hopefully, all our scholars will look back and reflect as they read this book, remembering what they were struggling with at this particular point in their lives and the progress they have made toward their life goals.

This volume should also be of interest to students considering enrollment at Ottawa University as they wonder what the life of the mind looks like in our neck of the woods. I can think of no better portrait of the potential that awaits our incoming students than this glimpse into the world of our Ottawa Scholars. Our Scholars are perceptive, motivated, funny, and brave. They have promising futures ahead of them, and are poised to lead lives of significance.

I know you will enjoy this third volume of *The Ottawa Scholar* as much as I have while working with the students to prepare it for you.

All the best,
Dr. Justin Clarke
Menard Family Professor of Philosophy
Director, Ottawa Scholars Program
Ottawa University Midwest
May 2022

FOREWORD

EDUCATION AND THE LIBERAL ARTS

*The following is the text of a speech I delivered to
the OUKS Community in Ottawa, Kansas,
during our Fall University Convocation on
August 18, 2021. – Dr. Justin Clarke*

Thanks for the kind introduction. I'm honored to address you today, and extremely dismayed to have to follow Dr. Tsutsui and Dr. Reggies.

Let me begin by saying that I'm thankful for the opportunity to be in the classroom again, to be on campus again, to be having face-to-face discussions with students and colleagues again. I'm thankful to be able to meaningfully participate in our community. I thought I'd say a little bit about a liberal arts education in general, and what I think makes our community special. But first, a cautionary tale.

When I was nine-years old, I was in Mrs. Owens' fourth grade class. I was in the middle of our table of desks, arguing with my friend and table-mate Brandon Cooper. I can't even remember what we were arguing about, except that I was firmly in the right. Anyway, I wanted Brandon to clarify something he said. I remember I said, "Be pacific." Brandon immediately stopped me.

"Spe-cific." He said. "It's with an S, not a P."

Oh no. I couldn't believe it. How embarrassing! My good friend Brandon was an idiot, but after I told him that, he wouldn't relent. He kept asking things like "Pacific like the ocean? Related to the ocean?"

Obviously not. Plenty of words sound similar to each other. *That's how words work, Brandon.* So I doubled down. I called Mrs. Owens over to have her explain—pacifically—how the English language worked to my friend.

Well, Mrs. Owens patiently and gracefully explained to the entire table that Brandon was in fact right, and I was wrong. I was the one who didn't know how language worked, and who was now beet red, embarrassed, and ashamed. It ruined my day, of course. I mean, it's 30 years later and I can still feel the heat of the shame.

And now I'm going to shamelessly rip off a point Kathryn Schulz made in a talk based on her 2010 book titled *Being Wrong*.[1] I'm going to ask you to think about some time when you were wrong—dead wrong—and think about that experience and what it *felt* like.

Please—really go back there—marinate in the feeling of being wrong.

Sometimes I ask my students to do this, and then I ask them to describe the feeling that they are marinating in. They often repeat some of the feelings I've just used to describe myself after I was thoroughly taken down a peg by Mrs. Owens. They say they felt *embarrassed*, they felt *stupid*, they felt *ashamed*.

But that's not what I asked you, or them, to imagine. I asked you to think about what it was like to *be* wrong—not what it was like to *find out* that you were wrong. And if we look back at my little story, we can see that I was wrong *from the beginning*. I was initially wrong when I used "pacific." I was wrong telling Brandon that he didn't know how the language worked.

How did I feel at *those* moments, when I was truly, objectively, wrong? Well, at those moments I felt amazing; I felt sure of myself. Because—and this is important—what does it feel like to be wrong? Well, it feels exactly like being right.[2] And so it was only *after* I felt so sure of myself, in fact, that I acted like a pretentious little jerk, that my own ignorance was revealed to all and I was promptly—and rightfully—hoisted by my own petard.

I'm done stealing from Kathryn Schulz. I'm now going to steal from some other people: dead philosophers, Bertrand Russell and Donald Davidson. It's widely conceded in philosophy that we are, each of us, wrong very often. And even though philosophers admit this, they usually think they are wrong *less often* than those *other* people, but this is actually just one of the things philosophers themselves are wrong about.

None of us is right about everything. It is just a simple feature of each of our individual sets of beliefs, that all of us believe

---

[1]Schulz, Kathryn. *Being Wrong: Adventures in the Margin of Error*. Ecco, 2011.
[2]This is the point that Schulz makes so effectively.

things that are just plain false. Further, we all *know* that some of our beliefs must be false. Nonetheless — *and this is the curious part* — we, by solitary introspection, are almost totally incapable of distinguishing our false beliefs from our true beliefs.

To believe something is *by definition* to think that it is *true*. It isn't as if we can just think really hard, isolate and inspect a belief on its own, and determine whether the belief is true or false. As Russell said, our beliefs don't come with some sort of tag or mark which we can check, and by means of which we can sort the true ones from the false ones.

No, to do this kind of sorting of our own beliefs, we need *other* people. In order to figure out whether the world really is the way that it seems to me, I need something more than my own "seemings," and this is where it pays to have somebody else to bounce my beliefs off of. I need to see if things *seem to you* the way they *seem to me*.

Even though we're inescapably fallible, there is actually quite a bit of good news here. If what I've just said is right, then in order to be wrong about *anything*, we have to be right about a lot more. Error and disagreement can only arise against a background of mostly true, and shared beliefs. Disagreement requires communication, and communication — mutual understanding — requires and presupposes a shared conceptual scheme that more or less corresponds to the way things really are.

What does this have to do with a liberal arts education? What is a liberal arts education anyway? There are as many defenses of a liberal arts education as there are definitions of a 'liberal arts education.' Everyone seems to agree that a liberal arts education is important and vital — necessary to the health of the republic even — while disagreeing about what it actually is.

Now if we look at the history of the term liberal arts, we find that the term's roots reach back to the Greeks and Romans, where an education that was 'liberalis' referred to a course of study befitting a respectable free subject. So I can now, finally, connect what I have been saying with the purposes of a liberal arts education, which is of course the type of education that Ottawa University strives to provide.

What befits a respectable, free subject? How does one even become a respectable free subject? I want to claim that in order to be really free, and really respectable, you have to both know and respect yourself. In order to know that you really are both the cause and author of your actions, you have to know what kind of person you are, and what you believe. And this isn't the kind of knowledge you can get by querying Wikipedia. To know who and what you are, and how and what you think, you need to be immersed in a community of other minds. College is a unique time and place where you are surrounded by other minds that are also trying to find out who and what they are, and how and what they think.

We know that we are fallible creatures, and that some of our beliefs are incorrect. And we also know that we don't know which of our beliefs are the incorrect ones. Furthermore, we know that the best way to find out which of our beliefs are true, and what our beliefs actually are, is to discuss them with others; others who, like us, are going through a similar process.

So what is the form a liberal education should take? I think the better question to ask is: "Given that we are striving to achieve a liberal education, what should our community look like?" I think we want to strive to be a community where we don't take a perverse pride in thinking we're right—that we've got it all figured out—because we don't.

We should strive to be a place where open and honest discussion, thinking out loud, and playing devil's advocate are all encouraged, and where finding out that you might be wrong is as painless as possible. We ought to be a community of individuals that actively seek out the opportunity to discover that we might be wrong, because that is the only way we are ever going to improve the leaky ship that is our current set of beliefs, and the only way to do this is to have friendly and honest discussions with people who disagree with us.

We should welcome careful agnosticism on polarizing issues, and not demand that others choose sides. We want our conversations—and, more importantly, our disagreements—to be guided by the principle of charity: to assume the best, and never the worst, about those with whom we disagree. As a community of respectable, free subjects, whatever in particular we disagree about, we want to see each other always as—in general—believers of the true and lovers of the good. It's my great hope that we, together, can provide this kind of community for each other.

And a final, quick, but hopefully comforting point. No matter how embarrassing finding out that you were wrong can be, no one remembers the times you were wrong with the kind of morbid intensity that you do. So not only should we extend grace and goodwill to others when they're wrong, we should definitely extend some of that goodwill back towards ourselves, as our own most severe critics.

Because, after all, I'm fairly certain Brandon Cooper is not somewhere, right now, telling a story to a large group of people about how Justin Clarke was wrong in fourth grade.

Unless, of course, I'm wrong about that.

SECTION ONE

Our first-year scholars wrote in response to the following prompt: "Why did you choose Ottawa University? What are you most looking forward to during your Ottawa experience?"

Our scholars come from all over, and they have many educational options. It is always interesting and affirming to read their reasons that led them to join our Ottawa community. Reading what our scholars see in OU helps us see ourselves with fresh eyes. This section reminds us that our incoming students have set the bar high, and it is up to those of us who comprise Ottawa University to meet their expectations.

This literary window provides an honest look into our scholars' lives and it is fascinating. I am excited to have such a talented group of students on campus for the next few years.

FAITH BEIKMAN

Reflecting back to my senior year in high school, I can say that having to make the decision where to go to college and invest the next four years of my life was one of the toughest decisions I have had to make thus far. There were so many unknowns, and the process of making a decision was quite scary. I started the decision-making process by asking myself what I wanted out of my college experience. I decided that a quality education, a sense of community, opportunities for personal growth, building relationships, playing volleyball, and having fun were important attributes that I was looking for in a college. I decided these attributes would help me succeed to the best of my ability and pave a way for my future. After considering each of these attributes, I knew attending Ottawa University (OU) was the right choice to achieve my goals.

One of the most important reasons I chose OU was because it provides a quality education in my field of study. I have a strong interest in elementary education and coaching volleyball, which OU provides. The number of students in each class is small, which is quite beneficial to learning and allows for better communication with instructors and collaboration with fellow students. There are also numerous opportunities for hands-on learning in various settings, which is helpful in gaining experience and clarity as I decide the exact educational pathway for me.

Already in the first semester at OU I had the opportunity to participate and learn in a preschool classroom setting. There will also be more opportunities in other areas relevant to the field of education in the future. In addition, the faculty is well credentialed and has diverse backgrounds and experiences in the education field, which provides great opportunities for learning. It is clear that each faculty and staff member in the education department is committed to student growth and success, and they demonstrate a passion for the field of education.

Another reason I chose to attend OU was that it allowed me to achieve my goal of becoming a collegiate athlete. Volleyball has been my passion for the last ten years and I wanted to continue playing the sport I love. I am competitive by nature and the OU volleyball program has historically been a strong contender in the

KCAC and NAIA, which is impressive. I am honored and excited to belong to such a great program. Competing on any team, but especially at the collegiate level, will help me develop many life skills, such as teamwork and collaboration, time management, a strong work ethic, commitment, dedication, and resilience. These skills will be helpful, not only with my college education, but later in life as well. Because going to college, being on my own, and meeting new people can be scary and stressful, I knew being on the volleyball team would provide a better opportunity to meet friends and be part of a family away from home.

Coming from a very small 1A high school with only 15 in my graduating class, I felt that a big university would be over-whelming. I like the feel of a smaller community, which OU pro-vides. It is small enough to offer a home-like and comfortable atmosphere, but large enough to offer diverse opportunities. I am able to get to know people with the same interests as I have, but I am also able to broaden my experiences and gain new interests. There are many ways to become involved on campus that will make my college experience more enjoyable and easier.

On my campus visit, I was told about different clubs and organizations that could help me meet people and fit my inter-ests. Some clubs and organizations that stood out to me were the Fellowship of Christian Athletes, the sororities, and more. Each student can find a club that fits their interests. Because most of the student body at OU are student athletes, everyone seems sup-portive of each other and cheer on other teams, which creates a fun and exciting environment. The entire campus seems to be a light-hearted and an enjoyable place to be. Like my hometown high school, everyone knows me and I know them. At OU, the faculty and staff know students by their name and take the op-portunity to get to know them personally. Making the decision to come to OU was easy because it offered a smoother transition as opposed to going to a larger university, and everyone here em-braces each other's differences and supports each other in their journeys.

As I start my college journey at Ottawa University, there are many experiences that I am looking forward to such as making new friends, playing volleyball and trying new things. There are so many freedoms that college provides that I am excited to experience. The most important thing I am looking forward to is making new friends. Coming from a small community, I have grown up with the same people my entire life. Although knowing everyone around me was comfortable and had its benefits, I am ready to meet new people with different interests. After experiencing a semester at OU, I can already say I have met some lifelong friends. However, I am looking forward to building upon those relationships and continuing to experience new ones.

As I said before, volleyball has always been my passion. By coming to OU, I was given the opportunity to build upon my skills and gain new knowledge of this sport that I never had. Already finishing a season at OU, I have improved my skills immensely and I am excited to learn more. Because I would like to become a coach one day, playing volleyball at the collegiate level will better equip me to teach my future teams to the best of my abilities. I am excited to see what my future playing volleyball at OU will teach me.

Lastly, by attending OU I am looking forward to trying new things. Since I attended a small high school, I was involved in a lot of the same activities from grade school through high school. Coming to OU will give me opportunities to participate in different activities that I have never experienced before, which will help me discover new interests and new people. The opportunities are limitless, and I am excited to see what OU has to offer.

Faith Beikman is a freshman from Linn, Kansas. She is majoring in elementary education with plans to teach upon graduation in 2025.

ZOE BUTTS

In order to comprehend the value of a liberal arts education, one must understand the core principles of such an education. Ottawa University is a liberal arts college. The goal of the University is to help students live a life of significance. A liberal arts education helps to build free thinkers and knowledgeable citizens. A liberal arts education allows students to learn and interact with ideas and people who are different than they are.

Liberal arts education was popularized in the mid-to-late 19th century when 212 schools were established between 1850 and 1899. Since then, there have been around 550 liberal arts colleges established in the United States. Their aim is to create students who are willing to consider options and opportunities that are outside of their normal realm of thinking. It creates opportunities for students to work with other cultures and backgrounds to create new ideas and understandings. In the classroom, the goal of a liberal arts education is to aid students in learning to work with others and to create a practice of mindfulness where other people's opinions and ideas are concerned, thus creating respectful and knowledgeable individuals.

Living a life of significance is done when people touch other people's lives in positive ways. A liberal arts education helps students prepare for a life of significance. It teaches them how to work with others and take other people's needs into consideration. In the Ottawa University education classes, we often discuss the different types of learners and how to adjust our teaching to the students' individual needs. If a student has ADHD or dyslexia, they will need to be taught differently than another student without those challenges. We learn about proper ways to adjust to the students and their unique ways of learning and comprehending material.

In the future, I look forward to using the skills I have learned in the classroom at Ottawa in my own classroom. My major is Secondary Education English and I plan to use this degree to teach Middle School Language Arts. My education at Ottawa University has taught me the importance of being open minded and considerate of other people. Eventually, I plan to have a classroom where every student feels welcome and safe. I plan to accomplish this by having clear rules and expectations in my classroom. Rule one for my classroom is that you are to respect your fellow classmates, the staff, and yourself. Rule two is listen to others and think before you speak. My philosophy is that the classroom should be a place where students feel safe to express themselves and not be afraid of being judged. Learning from other students and new resources is one way students can be positively impacted by the classroom setting. Liberal arts education teaches college students problem-solving skills and new ways to look at problems. It gives students perspective and allows them to learn and grow.

I am unsure of where I want to teach in the future. The options and possibilities are endless. Through Ottawa I have discovered that there is no one path that I have to follow. I've learned about many different career and life paths that I have the opportunity to take. I could teach in a different country or even simply a different grade level than I had originally planned. When I first started at Ottawa University, I thought I knew exactly what I wanted to do. I had planned to teach high school English—and only English—in my old high school. Now that I have gone through Ottawa and taken classes in different liberal arts courses, I have discovered a lot about myself and where my interests truly lie.

I have discovered that I enjoy History a lot more and plan to pursue a minor in it. I have also discovered many different genres and authors that I had never heard of or had the pleasure of reading. I plan to incorporate these authors into my teachings and allow students to have a broader access to literature. I have also discovered that I have a passion for writing stories. After graduating, I plan to continue this new discovered passion for writing and use it to create books and short stories. Without the classes at Ottawa University I would never have discovered the many different passions and interests I now hold.

While attending Ottawa, I have had the opportunity to take a wide variety of courses. One in particular that I enjoyed the most is Interpersonal Communication. This class allowed me to have a better understanding of how to communicate with others. It also taught us that communication is not always what we think it is. Body language, nonverbal communication, and other forms of communication all work together to allow us to get our message across. The class taught me that other people do not always communicate the same way I do and that this can be a tool rather than a problem or obstacle. Understanding how others communicate can allow us to build stronger connections and learn things we never would have immediately thought. I plan to use this in the future when working with students.

Some students may not communicate what they are thinking and feeling but this can be understood by looking at how they are behaving in the classroom, how well they work with others, and how they are performing academically. A problem that many teachers have is that they assume a student is failing simply because they are not trying their best. However, this is not always the case. We learned in class that there are many factors that go into determining why a student is struggling and we have to be able and willing to look for these signs. This is one example of how every class I have taken at Ottawa University has had an impact on my future and how I plan to perform in my future classroom.

One excellent part of attending a liberal arts college is the opportunity to learn about and experience other cultures. This last semester, the Whole Earth Club hosted a Swedish day in the cafeteria where students were able to try authentic Swedish food and learn interesting facts about Sweden. This occurs almost every semester with different countries on each occasion. At this year's Club Fair, students were able to try snacks from France, Sweden, and many different countries. The Whole Earth Club is only one of many ways that students can learn about different cultures and experience various cultural traditions. The Whole Earth club has also gone on short trips to renaissance festivals, and many different authentic restaurants with cuisine offering dishes from other countries.

Ottawa University also has had a few other events where students were able to learn about other cultures and lifestyles. On a student life day, Dr. Galiana taught the students about Buddhism and yoga. She not only presented that lecture but also offered a class about this as well. Informative and fun classes such as this one are some of the positive things about attending a liberal arts college. During one of the weekly student life days, students had the opportunity to attend a meeting about the many different travel opportunity experiences going on this year through Ottawa

University. These opportunities include a trip to Guatemala, Ghana, and Scotland. The school has hosted many trips in the past including trips to Ireland, Japan, and France.

This year Ottawa University has a liberal arts class titled "Tombs and Tales of Ancient Scotland." In this class, students are able to learn about Scottish culture and specifically the Orkney Islands. A main part of the class is that students are required to present a final project. This project is designed and created by each student, they are able to research and write about something that is of interest to them. The class ends with a trip to the Orkney Islands at the end of the semester. While in Scotland students get the opportunity to do hands-on research and finish their projects. I am looking forward to attending this class and making the trip this coming semester.

Another trip that I am looking forward to in the near future is the Music Department's trip to Chicago this spring. The choir and bands are going to be traveling to Chicago in March 2022 to enjoy multiple concerts and museums. It will be an excellent opportunity for the students to learn about different types of music and forms of art. We will have the opportunity to attend a play, view live bands and performances, as well as attending an opera. I am looking forward to learning and enjoying these many aspects of art. This is yet another positive experience that would not be possible without the school's goal of creating an environment where students can learn about the many different cultures and communities in our world.

Zoe Butts is a freshman from Houston, Texas. She is a member of the Braves softball team. Zoe is majoring in biology and expects to graduate in 2025. Following graduation, Zoe plans to apply to veterinary school and pursue a career in animal science.

JACKSON DAHM

Finding the right college to go to is always a hard decision. Location, cost, classes, major, and athletics are all things one has to consider. For me, however, it wasn't too difficult. Ottawa University had everything I needed in a college and more. I knew It was the right first choice for me after my first visit. Everything just seemed like the perfect fit. The scholarship and athletic opportunities were amazing. Coming from a family that had struggled with finances that was a huge blessing. Ottawa is only about three hours away from my hometown. I had an amazing opportunity to be part of the top scholar program and they offered the major I was interested in. It was a no-brainer for me to choose Ottawa.

The small size of the school was a huge factor for me. I grew up in Fayetteville, Arkansas and went to Fayetteville High School which had a student population of about 3,000. Often I would just feel like a number there and not a student who someone cared about. My experience at OU has been completely different. I'm not just another number to Ottawa. I'm a student, one who my professors know and care about.

One of the other major deciding factors in choosing Ottawa for me was the athletics program. I began wrestling my sophomore year in high school, but I never imagined I would have a chance to wrestle at the collegiate level, but Ottawa gave me that opportunity. It is so helpful to have professors and coaches who both understand and work with me being a student athlete. If schoolwork is too overwhelming I can talk to my coaches and get the assistance I need whether it be tutoring from someone or taking some time off practice if I need to focus on school. If I ever need anything I know I can go to my coach or any of my professors and ask.

Another great thing about the school is the small campus size. I never have to worry about running late to class because all of them are within a one-minute walk. I never have to worry about a long commute to class or practice. The class size is great as well at Ottawa. My largest class my first semester was only about twenty students. This is great because I really got to know my professors and classmates and it made it easier for me to learn with a smaller environment.

Towards the end of my first semester my engineering and physics professors had left for about a week. We did not have a professor to teach the class. I thought I would either have to retake the class or it would be offered online. However, Ottawa quickly found a replacement for both of the professors and I was able to finish the semester out normally. I can say confidently that if I had chosen to go to another school, I would have had to finish the class online.

The class variety is nice as well. I had the chance to take some classes I wouldn't think I could take or be able to take. The liberal arts education they offer is amazing. In my first semester I was able to take a class called "American Popular Music" which I wasn't too interested in at first but I needed a music class as a requirement. This slowly became my favorite class in the first semester as I was getting exposed to new music and learning the history of American music. I would not have had the opportunity to experience this had I not chosen Ottawa.

The friendliness of the staff and faculty is also unmatched. Everyone here interacts with each other like they have all been long-time friends. There is always something happening on campus. There have been so many fun activities and sports events in the first semester alone that it has seemed unreal. I have never *not* had anything to do during the year.

Ottawa was the right choice for me, I feel like I am home here. I didn't have that feeling of nervousness when moving in. It felt natural like just the next step in my journey. There's just an underlying sense that this is right for me based on everything on campus. In my time at Ottawa, I'm most excited to just see where I go and how much I learn. Being here, I feel I can become the best version of myself and I can't wait to take advantage of all the opportunities Ottawa has to offer.

The liberal arts foundation of Ottawa provides a great opportunity to branch out and explore other areas of study. I'm excited to become a part of the community and campus life, to meet new people and make friends. The people I have met are incredible whether that be my teammates, classmates, or just anyone I have interacted with. I feel I can really shine in Ottawa and improve both physically and mentally.

I am insanely grateful for the chance I have to be here and

wrestle. I am most excited about seeing where I can go athletically. Ottawa is providing me with all the tools I need to succeed in life. All I need to do is to take advantage of that opportunity. I'm excited to watch the campus grow as well. The new weight room being built onto the Mabee center is so exciting. Getting to be a part of a growing and evolving campus is amazing. I can't wait to see what else happens while I'm here. I know there are so many more incredible things to experience in college and I am beyond happy and excited that I am able to experience those things at Ottawa. I have absolutely no doubt in my mind that I chose the right college to go and receive my education.

Jackson Dahm is a freshman from Fayetteville, Arkansas. He is a member of the wresting team and is majoring in mechanical engineering. Jackson expects to graduate in 2025. Following graduation, he hopes to pursue a career in renewable energy.

BRENNA DILLER

Deciding where to attend college is a stressful and overwhelming task for most. Whatever decision to which a person arrives determines the experiences they will have for the next few years and dramatically influences their future and the person to whom they aspire to become. I found firsthand that choosing a school can be a daunting task. However, once Ottawa University was on my list of potential schools, my eyes kept gravitating to it. It encompassed all the characteristics I was searching for in a school.

At first, I was looking for a school close to home with a close-knit environment. It was important to me to be involved in a supportive community. The chance to play volleyball was a high priority for me. Receiving high-quality academic instruction was crucial. Ultimately, connecting all these elements through building lasting relationships was a significant component in choosing the college I would attend. Logically, all signs pointed to Ottawa. What ended up being my deciding factor was how much Ottawa University felt like "home." In the back of my mind, I knew that this is where I wanted to be, and when it came time to officially determine what school I was going to attend, it was clear to me that Ottawa University was the right choice.

As I mentioned, a school that provided a feeling of home was a vital consideration in choosing the college at which I would continue my education. It is very important to me to be close to home because my relationship with my family is very strong. I have three younger siblings that look up to me and I want to continue to play an active role in their lives. Since Ottawa University is only two hours away, it feels like the perfect distance to me. It is far enough away from my parents to live an independent lifestyle but still close enough that I can be involved in each of my family member's lives.

Also contributing to the reasons why Ottawa University feels like home is how similar it is to my hometown high school. I appreciate the small class sizes with personal connections to my professors and advisors. There was never a moment when I was exploring Ottawa University that I felt I would have a difficult time finding my way. The layout of the campus makes it easy to navigate. Even in aspects related to my development of a career, people are always there to answer questions and concerns.

Something that I have found to be even more true after starting my education here is that there is always a hand available to which I can reach out to for assistance. Not only is everyone available to aid me, but they also do it enthusiastically and with their best efforts. I can tell the staff members are not just doing their job but that they have genuine care and concern for each individual. I feel just as supported at Ottawa University as I do in my small hometown.

I have also been blessed with the opportunity to play volleyball for Ottawa University. One of my main goals coming out of high school was to attend a university where I could continue to be an athlete while getting a quality academic education. Some of my strongest relationships have come through being part of athletic teams. As a member of the volleyball team, it has been easy to form relationships with not only my teammates but also athletes across campus. There is always a game or event to attend to show support for each other.

While volleyball is important to me, even more important is being given the opportunity to prepare for "a life of significance," which is a pinnacle of Ottawa University and a pillar to which everyone involved with the university adheres. I enjoy having the opportunity to listen to speakers on Wednesdays to learn new perspectives on different religions and lifestyles. The housing staff in each building hosts events to relieve stress and promote social interaction frequently, which is a great way to experience positive interactions with new people.

I also feel I could build my life of significance at Ottawa University because of the opportunity I was given to become a Top Scholar. This program offers so many benefits to help students excel and there was no better way for me to do that than to attend Ottawa University. As well as being a Top Scholar, I have also become a student ambassador. Through this experience, I hope to display all the benefits of Ottawa University to potential students who are looking for the same traits in a college for which I was searching and help lead them to a "life of significance."

As I continue my education at Ottawa University, there are a multitude of things that I am looking forward to. I enjoy forming relationships and cannot wait to expand in this area. I am eager to experience the supportiveness of my peers. I look forward to furthering my academics to build my future. And finally, I can help other students find their home at Ottawa University. With it being a small school, there are more opportunities for building relationships.

What I love most about this school is the supportive atmosphere. Everywhere I go on campus, there is someone I know waiting to offer a smile or engage in genuine conversation. Building relationships comes easy here and that is what I appreciate the most. I am also eager to continue my academic experience. I have not yet taken a class that I did not enjoy or met a professor who does not continuously try to make the best experience for each of their students.

While I am receiving a great education during my time at Ottawa, this school opens doors for many avenues to matriculate. Although I have not yet completely decided on the career I would like to pursue, it is through the help and support of these relationships that I feel confident I will develop a career path that I love. After spending the first semester here, it reaffirms that I made the right decision and I look forward to continuing my education at Ottawa University.

Brenna Diller is a sophomore from Hiawatha, Kansas and is a member of the Braves volleyball team. Brenna is majoring in exercise science with a concentration in pre-allied health while minoring in leadership and management, and expects to graduate in 2024. Following graduation, Brenna plans to pursue hospice nursing.

ISAIAH EPP

The last year of high school is one of the most stressful parts of the lives of many. It serves as a stepping stone from childhood to the realities of adulthood, and then the transition into an ever-changing world. With new responsibilities and life decisions, the average person makes an incredibly important decision: whether or not to go to college. I had the option to go to trade school, be adventurous, and start a business, or just simply work at a factory. However, despite all those choices, I decided to go to college, which requires a whole batch of choices all by itself. I had to decide between hundreds of different colleges, examining their individual benefits and downfalls. Nevertheless, I chose Ottawa University because of its small community, a desired program, the beautiful campus, bountiful events, and its tireless march to get me ready for the future.

One of the beneficial aspects of a small college is its corresponding community which provides students with a rich environment where their professors are almost always available for them. The students do not have to worry about fighting for the attention of their individual professors as at some larger schools. This creates an intimacy within the community that most other colleges struggle to create where students meet most of our fellow classmates and teachers throughout the entire day. However, there are many small colleges throughout Kansas, so why did I choose Ottawa?

I initially saw that Ottawa had a jazz program, which is rare among small schools, and it had a rather good music staff as well. Jazz is my all-time favorite type of music, and going through life without it seemed impossible for me. So wanting a small school and a chance to study jazz further, I came to Ottawa. Nevertheless, my mind had not settled on whether I wanted to pursue jazz independently, or to follow a performance or teaching route instead.

College is about discovering one's self after all, so in due time I will know. There are many downfalls to a smaller music program, however, like a lower competition with other music students. Yet there are many benefits as well, such as the ability to talk to your professors freely. But even through the pros and cons,

Ottawa was still the right choice for me in my desired program.

Then, one cannot forget about the beautiful campus that the entire program is built upon. The aged trees that inhabit the campus give off a rather mystical feeling. They even complement the buildings that range from rather curious to gorgeous to rather complex. Where the oldest buildings give off a very studious aura, the newest buildings exude the warmth of the people who inhabit it. A person will not go wrong by deciding to take a lovely stroll across the campus; in fact, they will instead be incredibly delighted. I do not regret choosing this college in part for its campus, which is gorgeous, and one can never go wrong by wanting to be around the beautiful place that is Ottawa.

Inside this incredible campus is one of the college's most crowning achievements: the endless amount of events that happen all semester long. One of the most exciting activities the college offers is their esports program. I have not been a part of this program this last year, but I love the concept since one of my favorite games of all time is a fighting game (Super Smash Bros Melee). It's not just lovers of video games that get the events, there are events for everybody on campus. There could be tie-dye shirts one day, or a hot cocoa fest in the lobby the next. In fact, I have met a few people myself through these events, so they are definitely worth going to. At Ottawa University, the average student will never get bored.

As for me, I am looking forward to the opportunities and new relationships that await. There is nothing more exciting than an adventure, and college is definitely that, especially when I am taking my first steps out into my own independent world. New people surround me, and new opportunities present themselves. It is like reading a book, and then becoming part of the book where the adventure is at my own fingertips, and I make all of the decisions. College is a part of the grand story of life, where one thing leads to another. Everything I cannot see is what I am most looking forward to at Ottawa.

Although the story is not just mine to share, it is by God that I am able to stand here today. I can sit and write about how wonderful this college is, but without God's guidance I do not think I would have ever made it. One of the greatest opportunities that he gave me when coming here is the ability to preach the gospel. Despite the natural Christian nature of the college, this place does not attract very many devout Christians. So I know that God has not sent me here just to study for my degree, but to help those who are depressed, needy, and need love most of all. That is the greatest challenge that awaits me in this grand adventure, but I know that God is with me always.

Ottawa University enhances its small community through its degrees, the campus itself, its numerous events, and the innate ability to get its students ready for the future. The university's small community does itself credit by creating a learning environment that inspires all of its students. Then, the campus itself gives off its beautiful light every time we wake up in the morning. It is also a great backdrop for the amazing activities that appear throughout the year. Through it all, Ottawa knows exactly what it is doing. It is creating a place where students can evolve and go through their individual adventures. Where Ottawa begins, the future follows.

Isaiah Epp is a freshman from Hesston, Kansas. He is a member of the music program at Ottawa University, where he participates in jazz band, wind ensemble, and the pep band. Isaiah is majoring in jazz studies and music performance and expects to graduate in 2025. Following graduation, Isaiah plans to pursue a career in jazz performance and composition.

CLEO FELTNER

There was a time in my life when I felt what every typical high school senior feels; I was ready to feel like a true adult and experience the empowering feeling of independence. I was ready to get out of the town I loved but felt stuck in it. I was ready to find the real Cleo. But the thought of discomfort and *actually* being an adult sounded more and more dreadful as every college application deadline approached. I found myself trapped in a world of worry and panic because I had no plan for my future education.

Living in a world that offers multiple choices, choosing where to attend college is a terrible task for someone who hates making decisions (me). I always longed for someone else to make the decisions for my future. I thought that my parents, or anyone who had been experiencing life longer than me, could tell me what the right choice for my future was. Other's opinions and ideas began to bounce around in my mind, and if anything, it made my decision-making process much more difficult. The voices of others made me question every potential decision I had already made, but I will always be thankful for experiencing this. I now understand the importance of making decisions for myself and not others doing it for me. Choosing my next step was obviously never an easy task, but my first look at Ottawa University made every doubt disappear.

What I wanted was a new home, so when I thought about choosing a college that was the best fit for me, I thought about my high school. The most rewarding part of attending the same school since kindergarten was without a doubt the family that was created through education. Classmates became more than just peers, teachers became more than just mentors, and the school became more than just a building. I wanted my college experience to imitate the community that I grew up in. In my short hour-long visit to Ottawa University last year, it had already become my new home.

Although there were only a few faces to see around campus that day, there was never a missed wave, new hello, or "Welcome to Ottawa University!" This visit left no doubt in my mind that Ottawa has a mission to create a community and a family within its campus. My first semester also attests to this. Classmates of all ages are no longer just peers, but they have become new friends.

Professors no longer just preach their lectures and grade my papers, but they have become the ones who care the most about my education, my mental health, and how my day was actually going. They have become the sturdy bones of Ottawa University's college body. Each building is not just a building, but they contain seats that welcome new faces and growth. They have become the pillars of Ottawa University's community. I chose Ottawa University because of the community and family I knew would welcome me with open arms. It really was a simple choice and I have not been disappointed.

As if one decision isn't hard enough to make, part of growing up is encountering a world of newness that requires many decisions along the way. I am currently an undecided major, and although at times the stress of deciding my future career weighs on me, I am thankful for the variety of classes that are offered at Ottawa University. No matter what one's major is, Ottawa offers many opportunities to explore within the world of learning. As a student, I look forward to learning within many different course areas, and from many different perspectives of professors. I am extremely grateful that OU also allows their students to study the world around them. My second semester at Ottawa is already full of excitement and new adventures. Because of Ottawa's support in academics, I have the opportunity to take a course that also includes a trip to Scotland. Ottawa University has brought me the opportunity to travel, explore, and continue to learn.

OU is an entire support system. Students support every athletic team and professors support each student who enters their class. I am extremely fortunate to have already learned from wonderful faculty who care beyond academics. This has been the best part of my current Ottawa experience and I can say with confidence that there is no doubt I will continue to receive top-tier education and care. I look forward to many more book discussions and papers with Dr. Hazucha, continuing to find my voice in writing with Dr. Dinneen, and meeting more professors who will change my life just as these two already have.

I wanted to find the true Cleo, and Ottawa has given me the experiences needed to do so. I wanted to find my new home and Ottawa has already given me more than that. Ottawa has given me a support system, resources beyond measure, and the opportunity to grow. Ottawa University is home.

Cleo Feltner is a freshman from Lyndon, Kansas. She is currently undecided in her major but is interested in English and writing. Cleo expects to graduate in 2025. She is also undecided on her plans following graduation.

RYLEE FIGGS

In the fall of 2020, my life was full of uncertainties. Although the pandemic caused most of them, my college search was also a catalyst to the mixed feelings I had toward where I should continue my education. Since I was old enough to fit into a glove, I always knew I wanted to play college softball and pursue my childhood dreams of standing on a college field. However, my dreams went above and beyond playing the game I've loved all my life. While looking for a college, my biggest desire was to find somewhere that felt as close to home as possible.

Thinking about leaving my family and venturing into a new chapter in my life felt daunting, and pushed me to find a college that allowed me to feel comfortable about my decision. While visiting many colleges and weighing out my options, I always came back to the feeling I had while visiting Ottawa University. After leaving the campus from a visit, I kept explaining to my mom that I just knew that's where I belonged. Throughout the duration of my visit, I kept feeling the things that I yearned for. Ottawa University made me realize that I could have more than one home in my life, and from that day on, Ottawa would become my second home away from home.

From the feeling of security in a small town to the pride of competing and the academic resources provided, Ottawa University gave me the opportunity to pursue a college experience that I have always sought out. However, the feeling that rushed through me on my visit made the decision much easier for me. The environment of the campus, along with the people I met, gave me a sense of comfort that is only found in a home. That's when I knew that I had found the right place to begin the next chapter of my life.

Not only was I able to be in a place where I felt right at home, but I was also able to continue playing a game that has consumed my life for the past thirteen years. Softball has not only taught me how to have a competitive nature and allowed me the opportunity to meet so many people, but it has also taught me never to take anything for granted but instead to keep pushing no matter what kind of adversity I may face.

Being able to have the opportunity to continue my softball career at one of the best programs in the country was not only a blessing, but it was just the icing on the cake for why I should go to Ottawa University. Furthermore, having the chance to receive the honor of being a Top Scholar and be recognized for the hard work I put into my education throughout high school was another reason why Ottawa was the perfect fit. Being able to represent the university not only as an athlete, but also as a Top Scholar, is one of the best honors I have been granted.

After experiencing my first semester at Ottawa University, I can undoubtedly say that it has begun to build a life of significance for me. Like most first years of college, this semester was a rollercoaster of events and emotions. However, because of every up and down I experienced at Ottawa thus far, I have matured and begun to grow into the person I have always wanted to be. From early morning weights, to long nights of studying, and including the feeling before my first college gameday, Ottawa has taught me how to stay calm in situations where it would be easy to lose control.

Furthermore, it has shown me how valuable the individuals around me can be, and how much of an impact they can have on me. Ottawa has granted me the opportunity to connect with people and build friendships that will undeniably last a lifetime. The memories that I will keep with me throughout the rest of my life are now being made, and the experience that Ottawa has given me thus far has catered towards the memories. I have learned that hardships that are overcome bring with them some of the best moments, and I would have not been able to realize this without the people I have met at Ottawa.

Not only has the university brought my life significance, but the people who have come into my life because of attending Ottawa have definitely changed my outlook on numerous aspects of my life. They have taught me how to live every moment to the fullest, even if it is not the most enjoyable. Additionally, they have all made me remember to keep pushing forward, even when it's easy to fall into the adversity that comes in life.

Not only has Ottawa University granted me the opportunity to continue my education and my childhood dreams of playing softball, it has also allowed me to begin building significance in my life and start the next chapter. Looking back through all of the memories I have already made in just one semester makes me extremely excited for the rest to come. Being able to step onto the field with Ottawa on my jersey and represent all of my newly found friends while also continuing a passion I've had for so long brings me much joy and excitement.

What's more, being able to show my talents in the classroom while receiving recognition as a Top Scholar, and being a part of a published book, allows me to celebrate all of my hard work thus far. With all this being said, the biggest thing I am looking forward to throughout my experience at Ottawa is continuing to make my family proud and commend them for pushing me to be the best I can be in each aspect of my life. Without them, I would not have been able to make my dreams come true, and for that, I am beyond grateful. Ottawa has allowed me to begin a journey into a life of significance, while also being at a campus that feels just like home. The people, the town, and the atmosphere of Ottawa, Kansas have made me recognize that I can have more than one home in life and more than one family.

Rylee Figgs is a freshman from Topeka, Kansas and is a member of the Braves softball team. She is majoring in applied psychology and expects to graduate in 2025. Following graduation, Rylee plans either to apply to the Kansas University Law Program or pursue a career in criminal psychology.

MACY GREUTER

Ladies and gentlemen, buckle up your seat belts and get ready to learn the answers to the questions you have all been pondering: Why did Macy Greuter choose to attend Ottawa University, and what is she looking forward to in her upcoming years at OU? Look no further, your wish is my command.

Growing up, I had always heard stories about Ottawa University. This is the place where my parents met, dated, and got engaged. They told us stories about the choir tours, their friends, how they did in classes, their favorite professors (some still there today, like Dr. Mordy), and how the seniors would climb up and paint the Tauy Jones dome. It was their place of many memories.

Ottawa University was always on my radar, but the idea of going there did not seem realistic to me until my family moved to Kansas when I was in seventh grade. After we moved, OU Campus Ministries got in contact with our church and invited us to several events they offer for middle and high school students. Thoroughly enjoying the events, my sister and I started annually going to Labor of Love and Braving Discipleship. There we made new friends (some who attend Ottawa University with us today), fell in love with the campus, and gained our own Ottawa University memories.

When it came time to choose a college, Ottawa was always on my mind as an applicable choice. My sister had just chosen OU as her college two years prior. Since I did not want to make my decision for college simply based on comfort and how close it was to home, I decided to see what other campuses had to offer. Although I toured several other campuses and kept my mind open, I always circled back around to Ottawa University. To make sure I was not choosing Ottawa based solely on emotional thinking, I decided I would compete for the Top Scholars Scholarships and if I received one, the decision would be sealed. Obviously, one can put the rest of the pieces together. Ottawa University was the perfect place to continue my education; a place full of family legacy, memories, comfort, and friends. During my Ottawa University experience, I am looking forward to seeing how these next few years shape my life and future. I am excited to meet new people, develop as a person, and see where life takes me.

I have always known that I want to help people and communities. The National Organization for Human Services defines human services as a "broadly defined, uniquely approaching the objective of meeting human needs through an interdisciplinary knowledge base, focusing on prevention as well as remediation of problems, maintaining a commitment to improving the overall quality of life of service populations." This is exactly what I would like to do. I chose human services as my major and I am looking forward to working with my academic advisor, Dr. Fish-Greenlee, to further my education in human services to find the right career for me. I plan to continue learning, using the knowledge, advice, and wisdom given by my many Ottawa University professors long after graduation.

This upcoming semester, I look forward to several trips. In March, I am attending the music department's trip to tour Chicago. In May, I will go on the Scotland trip with Dr. Fish-Greenlee and Dr. Hazucha where we will tour the Orkney Islands. Our days will consist of hiking, sightseeing, learning the history the island has to offer, and completing a research project from the class we will take beforehand in the Spring. In June, I plan on attending the Albania trip with Chi Alpha. On our trip, we will learn about the culture while helping with projects in the community. I look forward to these trips and more OU trip opportunities in the future with great excitement.

I have already experienced the late-night Campus Activities Board events, meeting new friends in the dorms, sharing our anger at the ice-cream machine being down in the cafe, the home football games in the pep band section, the school spirit surrounding homecoming, the loving Chi Alpha family and atmosphere, working in campus ministries, and having the amazing opportunity to be a co-director for Braving Discipleship, as well as the late-night homework and cramming to get papers done and study for tests in the library. I wish to continue to have these experiences through the rest of my years at Ottawa University, with hopefully less procrastination so the homework won't be done so late at night and the papers and studying don't have to be crammed. Like most things, however, I waited to write this paper until the last minute—so maybe not.

College is an interesting time in one's life. It is a mysterious and magical space between high school and adulthood. Everyone is attempting to piece their life together, hopeful for success. I know these next couple of years won't be incredibly easy, but I look forward to the experiences and knowledge that OU has to offer within the community of staff, history, and peers. I will try to live to the fullest while finding out who I truly am. I am excited for the years to come.

Until the next procrastinated paper – Macy Greuter

Macy Greuter is a freshman from Topeka, Kansas and is a member of the Braves music department. Macy is majoring in human services and expects to graduate in 2025. Following graduation, Macy plans to apply her degree with a career in human services.

NICHOLAS HATFIELD

For me, college was the next step in my journey towards developing my uniqueness and identity. As a twin, I have always been one of a set. My college goal was to find a place to expand my knowledge and establish who I truly am. The result was me taking a very different path from my twin brother. I was looking for a place to call home. When I sat down to evaluate my options of where I wanted to go to college, it came down to the people, the opportunities, and where I felt I belonged.

When looking at colleges, I quickly eliminated large state schools such as Kansas State University, Emporia State University, and Fort Hays State University. Even though these schools supported my degree path, sitting in a lecture hall with hundreds of other students would cause me to lose out on being able to personally interact with my professors and teachers. That did not appeal to me. I knew that Ottawa University was the place for me when I attended a campus visit.

I was impressed with the faculty and administration I met with during my visit. Specifically, what impressed me was how engaged they were in my educational journey and what I was looking to get out of my degree. The experience was the same whether meeting with Dr. Wenyika and Dean Anderson to my degree discussions with Dr. Carrier and Professor Lafikes. Each interaction was an exploration of my educationl journey and how the people of Ottawa University would be there to support me as I worked toward my goals.

The ability to further explore different topics and have in-depth conversations is invaluable. While at Ottawa University, I have gotten to know my professors. The small school environment provides the very best student-to-professor ratio. It allows for a direct student-to-professor relationship. The ratio allows for students to experience learning at different levels. If I do not understand a concept, there is time to revisit a topic or ask for a one-on-one explanation for clarification. If I want to go deeper or explore a topic, the professors and instructors are passionate about their areas of focus. This means I can explore the topic, and instructors make time for me. My passion for knowledge is encouraged to grow wherever I turn.

It is my goal to become a physical therapist. I have a passion for helping people stay active and maintain their physical independence. For a long time, this has been my goal. You see, I am a lucky person. All four of my grandparents have been an active part of my life growing up. I have seen what time does to them and their mobility. Keeping them active and maintaining their ability to get around were important to me. Helping others get the opportunity to play ball in the yard with their grandparents or getting to enjoy special moments fuels my desire for my career. As a physical therapist, I know I can make a difference in the lives of the elderly to keep them active and mobile.

When I explored degree options at other small schools, Ottawa University stood out among the rest. The combination of prep classes and practical experience will prepare me for physical therapy school. The opportunities for real, hands-on learning opportunities bring all the classroom work into a real-world experience. The Ottawa University program offered me to learn about topics needed for an exercise science degree and takes that a step further, allowing me to experience it as well.

The final area in my decision to select Ottawa University is proximity to home. Most high school seniors look forward to striking out on their own in a new place. However, I am a bit of an introvert. I like places where I feel at home and can make close friendships. The same feeling of belonging I felt when out and about in my hometown community is what I feel at Ottawa University because the university is part of my community. The people I see around Ottawa are the same people I see on campus. I make it a point to learn their names and they know me by mine. Ottawa University alumni are family members, people who attend my church, and friends of my family. Their experiences at Ottawa were ones that I wanted to experience as well. It also does not hurt that campus is less than twenty minutes from home so if I want to eat a homemade meal or forget something, I am only a short trip away. What's more, family members are free to drop off college care packages if they happen to be in town.

As excited as I am about my field of study and learning all I can about exercise science, the new friends and connections I am making in college are what I look forward to establishing. Ottawa University has all the benefits of a small school but with a very global and diverse student population. As I stated before, I am an introvert by nature. Going into my freshman year, I decided I needed to make a big effort to be more social and get to know more people.

After arriving at Ottawa University, I set my sights on meeting new people. Ottawa University's orientation weekend was a large part of spring boarding me into being more social. I have already met many different people from all over the country at Ottawa and I plan on continuing to make these personal connections and lifetime friends. Knowing that students come from all over, I wanted to meet new people despite being the introvert I am. I wanted to discover new experiences and make new friends from across the globe. Although it is outside my comfort zone, meeting new people is quite exciting because it shows how just a couple hundred to five thousand miles away can change everything about someone. Each person you come in contact with at Ottawa University brings their own experience and personality to school. In the end, we are richer when we take advantage of these connections.

The final area I am looking forward to at Ottawa University is a bit of a surprise for me. In middle school, I joined the cross-country team. At the beginning of my running career, I did not know how much of an impact daily running would make in my life. I have found over the last eight years of running cross-country and track that it keeps me healthy physically but mentally as well. Competing in my senior year of high school, I was sad to think my competitive running days were soon ending. However, after talking with Coach Scott and Coach Whittaker, I found a place on Ottawa University's cross-country and track teams. Ottawa University facilitates a vibrant atmosphere of athleticism, which fits my standards perfectly. Competing at the collegiate level is a little intimidating. I thought that the fourth and fifth miles of my first five-mile race were going to kill me, but the experience of a team and comradeship is that of a family.

My ultimate decision to become an Ottawa University Brave was based on the curriculum and degree path I wanted to pursue. However, I know my path to becoming a physical therapist is not just about the course work and the classes I take. It is about the people and the experiences which enrich that learning. I plan on doing this through joining clubs, studying, practicing with my teammates, and discussing and involving myself with other students of a similar or identical degree fields. I am looking forward to my time at Ottawa University to further my knowledge in the medical field while broadening and sharpening my interpersonal skills. In the end, I am looking forward to the holistic experience at Ottawa University to help shape me as a person who happens to be pursuing an exercise science degree for a career in physical therapy.

Nicholas Hatfield is a freshman from Pomona, Kansas and is a member of the Braves cross-country and track team. Nicholas is majoring in exercise science and expects to graduate in 2025. Following graduation, Nicholas plans to pursue a career in physical therapy.

MACEY MORRIS

Choosing a college is a tough decision for some students, partly because the college that we choose will become our second home. It is always hard to think about leaving home and starting a journey somewhere new, but this is exactly what seniors are asked to do when applying to colleges and making their campus visits. To be completely honest, Ottawa University was not my first or second choice. My initial choices centered around softball; I knew I wanted to play softball because I love it and was not prepared to let it go. I did visit Ottawa, and I loved everything about it, especially the softball program; however, after I had visited many different colleges trying to find my second home, I thought that I would rather stay in Oklahoma to be closer to my family.

Although I loved Ottawa's campus, its family-oriented at-mosphere, the coaches, and the buildings and dorms, I still thought that a four-hour drive was too far for me to handle. Four hours—that was the only thing holding me back. Thankfully, I overcame that mental hang-up. Now, after finishing my first semester, I have met many new people at OU, I have also realized that a four-hour drive is nothing compared to the distance that most of the students attending OU are from their friends and family, and I will never take those four hours for granted again.

Looking back a year ago towards the beginning of my first semester of my senior year, I committed to Seminole State Community College to play softball. The campus was not as nice, but I knew that a thirty-minute drive sounded like a better option for me at the time. However, due to internal financial reasons, unfortunately my scholarship was pulled, leaving me in complete shock. I felt betrayed, hurt, and at a loss for my future academic and athletic career. My main concern was to overcome this obstacle and my wounded emotions. I knew my future mattered more than my immediate emotions, so I immediately called Coach Shaffer from Ottawa and explained the situation.

She told me that my scholarship still stood, and also told me that I needed to put a portfolio together and apply for the Top Scholar competition. The hurt that I was feeling was a distant memory because of what coach Shaffer said to me. Shortly after having that conversation, I sent in a portfolio to the school and was accepted to attend the competition. I continued to go on visits and went to the competition. While I was on my way back from a visit, I received a call that I had received a scholarship from the Top Scholar competition.

I was over the moon excited, so much so, that a couple days after receiving that information, I verbally committed to Ottawa University. Not only my coaches, but also the University made me feel welcomed and happy. If I had never met my coaches or known of OU, I do not know what college I would have attended, what education I would have received, or if my dreams of playing college softball would have come true. I will forever be grateful for the kindness that was shown towards me, and I will never forget it.

What do I look forward to during my experience at Ottawa University? When I first arrived at Ottawa, I was extremely home-sick as most freshmen are. I started out going home every weekend, which kept me from pushing myself to make new friends and enjoy my time at OU. My mom ended up telling me not to come home every weekend because I was keeping myself from both meeting new people and allowing myself to have a good time. After I began to make new friends, I started to love OU so much more.

There are many things I look forward to for the rest of my journey here at Ottawa University. I look forward to meeting many more new people, making lifelong connections and friend-ships. I love making new friends and socializing with people I have never met before. Moving forward, I am looking forward to spending more time on campus and getting involved in cam-pus-wide activities that can push me to be a better leader as well as a better person. Ottawa University has already helped me grow as a person, and I cannot wait to see what all it brings me in the future.

The major that I have chosen to pursue is elementary ed-ucation. Nothing interests me more than becoming a teacher and a coach. OU has helped me learn to love the profession I have chosen so much more than I already had. I expect nothing less than to fall in love with my major and the teaching profession class that I will be taking next semester. What I most look forward to at Ottawa is to excel in the classroom while also excelling personally and growing mentally and emotionally.

When it comes to thinking about my future, Ottawa is a very important factor. Even though I have only spent one semester at OU, I can tell it will play a big role in shaping many futures because it has already started to shape my own. Softball has always been an important part of my life and Ottawa has allowed me to keep softball a priority while also prioritizing my future academically.

When I graduate, I want to be a teacher for grades K-8, as well as a softball or track coach. I have always wanted to be a softball coach, and Ottawa has the courses that can help me achieve those dreams. I intend to obtain an amazing experience and education out of Ottawa University that will then lead me to obtaining a good job that will help me start my life beyond school.

In all reality, Ottawa University will be a place where my personality grows, and my future starts to come together. This will be the place where I learn how to become the person that I am meant to be and pursue the dreams I have had, while finding new dreams to pursue. Growth is something so important, and OU is one of the best places to experience growth. In less than a year, I have discovered so much about myself and have experienced immense personal growth. Imagine where an entire year, or even four years will bring me. Ottawa University has gifted me with so much thus far, and I cannot wait to see what is to come.

Macey Morris is a freshman from Stroud, Oklahoma and is a member of the Braves softball team. She is majoring in elementary education and expects to graduate in 2025. Following graduation, Macey plans to become a teacher and a softball or track coach in her native state of Oklahoma.

EZEKIEL REAZIN

"Head east on East 13th Street, you will arrive at your destination in 35 minutes." This was the start to the next chapter in my life. My knees were bouncing in the passenger seat. My nerves never really got to me but this interview was scaring me, I had no idea what to expect. I was on my way to Ottawa for the Top Scholars interview.

Before this day, I had been to Ottawa a few times when our high school football teams had competed there. I liked that Ottawa was close to my hometown, Eudora, but was far enough away for me to explore and refine myself. Ottawa also has my ideal enrollment size where I knew I could present my ideas and they would be shared to the whole student population. This was a compelling selling point because I enjoy putting in my input from a student's point of view and know that it can help improve the whole school. I knew that I could do this here after I finished my interview.

During the interview process, I had the pleasure of talking with the Ottawa President, Reggie Wenyika, who gave me a little insight into all the great opportunities that Ottawa offers to help us make a difference and improve ourselves. Dr. Wenyika impressed me with his personal background and Ottawa's desire to improve a student's global perspectives. I also enjoyed talking with all the professors. Talking with them made me want to take more classes outside of what I needed just to hear more about the subjects because they had so much passion and enthusiasm. At Ottawa, the desire to learn and share ideas was obvious and I wanted that to be part of my personal growth.

After getting there, I realized how much I enjoyed the campus set up. I love how I can get to all my classes within five minutes of my dorm room and it is not all spread out. I also enjoy seeing my professors because I have time before and after class where I can actually talk to them. They each have a genuine interest in not only my education but also spending time talking about my thoughts and concerns.

Before I came to Ottawa, I had an idea of the degree that I would likely pursue—a business major. As part of my selection process, I knew I also wanted a school that encourages diverse thinking to make a person well-rounded. I wanted a business degree that was robust where I could enroll in religion, English, history, and other classes. A business degree is great but is more profound where you can engage in a variety of conversations. I was looking for a college that would encourage this well-rounded approach and Ottawa produces well-rounded graduates.

In the summer after the interview, I started training for football. At first. I was hesitant because it was different and I did not really know anyone. I would run around to all the different meetings and workouts just trying to keep my head above the water. Since then, I have really gotten to know the program and my team. At Ottawa, each team member really cares and wants to see each other succeed. They all check on each other to make sure they are up and ready for weights in the morning and they make sure that each one is getting the support we need in class. We did not have a successful record, but it was a success to see our team improve and bond.

In the fall, I took several business classes to apply towards my degree. There was an adjustment with the amount of home-work but I was never on an island fending for myself. The teacher gave informative lectures and provided lots of support for assign-ments. Plus, it was nice to get to know my professors and they took the effort to get to know me. I am more than a number to them. They make me feel like I am worthy of their investment and I sense that they want to see me flourish.

I'm looking forward to seeing what I can do to improve the experience for students similar to what I did in high school. In high school, I got to help with building a group that got the students and community more involved with supporting the school. I want to look into getting more involved with all the programs here at Ottawa and try to do the same. The main focus of the pro-gram is to get my fellow students and friends to come out and be supportive. I want to see every student section full for all of the athletes we have at Ottawa. I also want to see the university grow with the community that it has been a part of for so long.

I'm confident that Ottawa was the right choice after ex-periencing my first semester. I was always told that college is an investment. I would no longer be doing school because I had to.

I would attend college because I wanted to apply my degree so I could expand my job searches and set up for a more prosperous career track. I knew I made a good decision with Ottawa after an interview for an internship. As I was sitting there I found out that the interviewer went to Ottawa, which helps me out a lot. That's when I realized that I wasn't just getting a degree, I was making connections. Connections have helped me get to where I am. I'm so appreciative of everyone I've met because I know I can count on them to help me and, if they need me to help them, I will because I am a proud Ottawa Brave.

Ezekiel Reazin is a freshman from Eudora, Kansas and is a member of the Braves football team. Zeke is majoring in business economics and expects to graduate in four years. Following graduation, he plans to apply to Kansas University and enroll in the MBA program there.

ANGELO REYES

My name is Angelo Reyes and I am a first year student at Ottawa University. When I visited Ottawa, I had an overwhelming sense of that hometown vibe, despite this being a college town. It's definitely smaller, which I enjoy because I come from a small town. Another reason for the vibe would be the people; everyone has a good vibe to them. Visiting different schools, I could really see how people treat others and a lot of places do not treat everyone well. However, while at Ottawa, from the hotel staff to the school staff, everyone was nice and really willing and eager to help out in any way.

My stay here so far has been very rigorous with heavy involvement on my part. Being a business student, I have had to write many papers, learn some difficult (to me, at least) math, and learn what goes on in the micro/macroeconomics world. In fact, my favorite classes so far have been the micro- and macroeconomics ones. They were difficult but I enjoyed learning about the different topics involved that I had questioned in the past. Every professor I have come across has been overly helpful, whether that involved taking their own time to go over topics I was struggling with or making the classes more student-oriented.

While I committed to Ottawa, I believe it was really the school who picked me. The Top Scholars program was the best thing that could have happened. I do not come from money, so attending this private college would have put me in a major amount of debt. However, being able to become a part of the Top Scholars Program and receive an overwhelming amount of paid tuition made it possible for me to even be here. During the competition, that was my first look at the campus. I loved the size and build of Ottawa; being told how small the class sizes were by people who were already a part of the program was very helpful. I would not feel comfortable in a large class setting, especially if I was having difficulties. Meeting the staff and having the opportunity to sit down with the president was extraordinary.

Dr. Reggies made me feel a part of a family, remembering my name immediately. Whenever I see him around campus, he asks me how I am doing and if the wrestling program is doing as well. I don't believe this would happen at a large college, for everyone here makes themselves out to be real people, treating everyone else with the same amount of respect. Ottawa University makes a point to get people here and keep them here. The number of alumni who came back to help showed me how friendly and great this place is, so much so that people want to come back and pay forward what the university has done for them. Meeting a lot of people who had nothing but good things to say about the university really put the nail in the coffin for me. Seeing how happy people were to be a part of something so great made me want to be a part of this program as well.

What I'm looking forward to during my stay here in Ottawa is to grow mentally, not just academically or physically. I want to be able to meet and have a conversation with as many different people as possible. Being from a small town where everyone pretty much knew one another, I feel as if I was unable to grow mentally. A lot of people from outside of Kansas and Oklahoma attend this university. Even people from outside the U.S. go to OU, and that amazes me. I'm more on the quiet and non-talkative side, but I've talked to people who thought the same of themselves and have come out of their shell way more than they would have expected. While I must make the effort to make those friendships and acquaintances, I'm excited to see who else sees me as a person to talk to or confide in.

I'm looking forward to finding who I want to be in this life, outside of wrestling and school. I am nervous because I don't know what I want to be or have an exact profession I want to pursue. Yet the more I've been here, the more I learn that it's okay for not a lot of people know what they want to do until their second or third year. Some people have said even in their senior year, they're not sure of exactly what they want. I love the experience of learning something new, and the classes Ottawa provides are exactly what I'm looking for. My first semester I took all classes that contribute mainly to business, but for my second semester, my advisor helped me pick out classes that contribute to my understanding of psychology and fitness education. While I was afraid that taking different classes might affect me in the long run, she assured me that taking them would not hinder what I want to achieve and could even help me in many different jobs.

I am looking forward to what I can become here. The best thing I have been learning is that opportunities are everywhere. I just have to take them and run, whether that be learning or in the physical attributes. Being able to work in classrooms where I can make academic strides, as well as in a wrestling room where I can make those mental and physical strides, are great opportunities. Wrestling has always been a big part of my life, and this program seems like the best fit to progress in that discipline. That is another reason I chose Ottawa, the wrestling program has been an amazing experience. It has come with a lot of ups and downs but I have realized the best way to learn is failure so I can get it right. This has taught me that in life I can be whatever I want, but life will have its ups and downs. I am at peace with my decision to come to Ottawa University, and I am excited and ready for what comes along with that decision.

Angelo Reyes is a freshman from Shawnee, Oklahoma and is a member of the Braves wrestling team. He is a business administration major and plans to graduate in 2026. After graduation, he will apply to a technology center to further his knowledge in carpentry and masonry, or to intern on a job site.

BAYLER RINDLISBACHER

In my young life, I have come to learn that in almost any social situation, one person or group is always being judged by another. We can see this problem very early in life and we can all probably think of a painful childhood memory that confirms this. When we are young, we are judged for trivial things that seem important at the time, but ultimately are temporary. However, as we transition into adulthood, society's judgments become crucial and inescapable. Take for instance, a reformed convict who is thrown back into an unforgiving world, or take a person of color who deals with micro-aggressions on a daily basis. No matter what you do, someone is always there to judge you unfairly or to categorize you into a stereotype they think you belong to. Judgments that people make of us can directly impact your lives and often times we can't change them.

Yes, throughout our lives we are judged, but we also judge others. When we are children our judgments of others are based on what our parents teach us so we too learn to put people in categories. When we grow older, our perceptions of others are influenced by our jobs, media, and political leaders. It seems that being a young adult in college is one of the only times when we can ignore societal stereotypes and abandon preconceived notions of others.

In college, we can meet people from various walks of life and learn about unique cultures and histories. This is why it's so important to choose a college that welcomes diversity and has an open and judgment free atmosphere. Ottawa University is just such a place. OU offers the most incredible array of cultures, knowledge, and experiences I have ever had access to. Being from Utah, I have had a minuscule amount of exposure and have been given the chance to widen my lens at Ottawa.

During freshmen orientation week, we were privileged to hear from the chief of the Ottawa tribe of Kansas. She taught us about the tribe's history and how it is woven into the spirit at Ottawa University. She also took the time to welcome us as new members of her tribe. This introduction to college made me want to learn so much more about the people around me and the culture they brought to this school. It also made me feel comfortable with the culture I brought to the school. From day one, Ottawa has created a safe place for cultural experiences and ideas to be shared and appreciated.

As the fall semester came to a close, I reflected on my first semester of higher education and naturally, I thought of some of the people I met. I noted that three people were Jewish. This may seem insignificant, but I realized I had never met a Jewish person before beginning my time at Ottawa, and this astonished me. I met and spent time with members of a religion and culture I had never met before and I didn't even think twice about it. It wasn't because I lacked awareness, it was because I truly learned to see people for who they are.

At Ottawa University, we don't sort people into any type of categories. We accept people for who they are and everything they bring. The students here don't have to try and fit in anywhere. We excel by simply being ourselves. Anyone who comes to Ottawa University in any capacity can see we are a gigantic melting pot of ethnicities, religions, and cultures. However, at the end of day, we are all Braves.

Bayler Rindlisbacher is a freshman from Utah who is a member of the Braves baseball team. He is majoring in business administration and expects to graduate in 2025. Following graduation, Bayler plans to pursue management positions in the healthcare field.

ELLISE ROMINE

I began my journey of figuring out how to answer the question of "what comes next after high school?" with what I'd call a junk drawer full of possibilities. Everything I thought about pursuing was purely hypothetical and had no weight of passion behind it. This, at the time, was slightly alarming because all my classmates were tying together all the loose ends of their high school careers, wrapping them up into a nice ball of yarn that they could carry and use throughout their well-planned-out college years. I'm sure there were a lot of youth in my situation, not really knowing exactly what they wanted to do when college applications came around or even what they wanted the rest of their lives to look like. I happened not to know many of them, leaving me feeling alone, like I was falling behind, and a bit scared of what would actually come next.

The high school I attended, Washburn Rural, is large for a Kansas high school, which made it an easy place to find a decent-sized group of people who were as nerdy and excited about learning as I was. We had extremely exciting social lives, if you are wondering, living the life of packing in as many extracurriculars as humanly possible and trying to out compete each other for academic awards of excellence. We were quite the party animals, tearing up the quiet library study rooms during lunch period, waking up to drive to debate tournaments at 5 a.m. on a Saturday, or comparing notes on who found the best ACT study book. Surrounding one's self with people who are like this means that 98% of the people around us have had a plan A, B, C and D about their post high school life — not to mention that each plan has their own sub-plans and then those sub-plans have their sub-plans, and so on.

These extremely put together kids were a whole different level of intimidating, especially when it was the January of my junior year of high school and they are already going on and on about how excited they are after submitting their early admissions applications to whatever Ivy League school they were interested in and peer editing their fifth rough draft of their college essays. I had not even thought about college applications at this time, let alone the dreaded admissions essays. Instead of joining the bandwagon and addressing my stress about what I was going to do once high school was over, I just brushed it off and procrastinated until my senior year began. I had haphazardly applied to a few schools by the time August rolled around, but it was mainly just state schools where all you have to do is click a few buttons, toss an application fee at the school and then, bam! You are in. Real heavy lifting if you ask me. I also had not even decided on a profession. I had tossed around the thought of being a lawyer or a business woman but only because of the possibilities of making a lot of money, and I figured that I was probably smart enough to work it out.

While I was still "working it out" (which is code for ignoring my problems) alongside the very few others in the AP and IB programs who were in the same situation as I, I happened to stumble upon a new idea of how I could answer "What comes next?" During my junior year of high school, Kansas sanctioned girls wrestling, which was a sport I had participated in a bit when I was younger, but had abandoned it when I entered high school. That way I could slot in another extracurricular activity that I, at the time, thought would look more appealing on a resume. I decided to rejoin the sport because I figured if it was sanctioned while I was still in high school that it must be a sign from up above. In reality, it was probably not a sign, but I had been purging out a lot of the extracurriculars I had been packing into my schedule because I decided I really did not care about the elusive *resume* that I must pack full with things I didn't really care about doing.

I was feeling burnt out at the time so the thought of doing something different that I had found fun in the past sounded refreshing. It turned out that I did actually really like it, *and* I was not half bad at it either. I was decent enough to catch the interest of Coach Mahdi during my senior year who, at the time, was the head coach of the women's wrestling program at Ottawa. He contacted me early on in the school year before the season had even started and was the one who introduced me to the Top Scholars program. Mahdi put his full confidence in me and believed I could secure a good scholarship through the program. He also did a really good job of getting me interested in both continuing my athletic career and also his program. So I submitted a portfolio to the program and looked forward to seeing what the Ottawa University campus was all about.

My first time visiting the campus was the day of the Scholars competition, and my absolute first thought was "this is tiny." In fact, Ottawa University is so small that it takes up a lovely two square blocks and the student population is less than half the size of my high school. I was actually put off by this since I was used to being at a much larger school and surrounded by a lot of people. I did not come to like it until I'd been living on campus for a few weeks, and now it is one of my favorite things about Ottawa for a few reasons.

First, on a small campus, everyone will know you and you will know everyone. In high school, I was used to only being recognized by others in the programs and groups I was already a part of. People always think large schools make it much easier to meet new people left and right, but students really end up only being noticed by people who already know them and tend to be ignored by those who don't. I'd actually say that the larger a school is, the harder it is to branch out because there is so much happening all the time that it blurs into one big mess and it becomes easier to stick to what you already know. What's more, my class sizes were always huge and most of my teachers would see hundreds of different students a day in their classrooms, making it easy to be glossed over. On a smaller campus, the blurriness goes away and it's easy to see the crowd as individual people, making it easier to talk to everyone on campus and to get a more individualized education as the class sizes are smaller. There is no going unnoticed on this campus.

Second, I can stroll across the whole campus at a leisurely walking pace in about five minutes. This may seem insignificant to most people, but to me it means I can masterfully pull off waking up ten minutes before class, rolling out of bed eight minutes before, leaving three minutes until class begins and arriving with a whole minute to spare. I'm not going to personally recommend this method to anyone else, but it's a huge plus to living on a small campus.

The Top Scholars competition gave me a good insight into Ottawa's mission and educational expectations, and allowed me to learn more about what a liberal arts education is. The competition also introduced me to almost every professor at the school and allowed me to get to know each of them a bit. Overall, it was a pleasant experience and for the first time that school year, the anxiety and stress I had been feeling about what would come after high school was gone. Regardless of how the competition would end up for me, I had a gut feeling that Ottawa was right for me, and I even remember telling my mom as much as we were walking back to the car that afternoon.

I came back to campus the week after the Top Scholars competition to meet the women's wrestling team and the visit, primarily meeting with my future teammates, confirmed my feelings I was having about Ottawa being the place for me. When I reached the financial office at the end of my visit, my mom and I were told to sit tight. After about ten minutes, Mr. Otto burst out of his office and told me that I had received the presidential scholarship. I was shocked, and may have *possibly* cried at this news, because I was expecting to get this information in the mail in about two or three weeks, not surprised with the information five days after the competition in an office surrounded by people. They had my mom and I wait in the lobby because they were frantically trying to finish the scoring of the competition because they "had a good feeling about me." I guess they were right because I got the scholarship and by the end of my financial meeting, I had already accepted the scholarship and committed to the school. In the end, I had a good feeling about the school and the school reciprocated, making it a seamlessly perfect college match.

I've been at Ottawa University for a semester wrestling and studying art education, and have enjoyed every day of it. I can confidently say that I've grown as a person, student, and athlete over the past few months and look forward to continuing this growth over the next three years. I've never felt more sure of the fact that I'm on the right path in life than right now, which is the polar opposite of where I was a little over a year ago. I am no longer a stressed-out, seventeen-year-old who is fretting over whether or not I have the next ten years perfectly mapped out. I am a young adult who is excited for all the loose ends of the future, letting whatever happens happen, and who isn't scared of what comes next because every day, I'm surrounded by great people at a great institution who are here to help me navigate life. Ottawa University has become my home for the next four years and I wouldn't want it any other way.

Ellise Romine is a freshman from Topeka, Kansas who is majoring in art education and expects to graduate in 2025. Following graduation, Ellise plans to apply to a master's program and pursue a teaching career at the secondary level.

LINDI SCHMELZER

My whole life I have been a goal-oriented person. Everything I did was for a purpose and everything I did in high school was to further my education when I graduated. Once I was a quarter through of my senior year, I was constantly asked questions about where I was going to college and what I was going to do. My answer, ever since my freshman year of high school, was the same. It was the same until I visited a small university in Ottawa, Kansas that instantly changed my mind. There were a lot of reasons that I chose Ottawa University as the place to further my schooling, but there were two main ones: the golf team and the town itself. Ottawa was also a far enough distance from my parents where I wouldn't have to see them every day, but close enough that I could go home for the weekend if I wanted to. I knew Ottawa University was the perfect fit for me and I could not be happier with my choice of schools.

The biggest reason I chose Ottawa was its golf program. Growing up, my dad and I were always out on the course. I always prioritized other sports over golf though, such as softball and basketball. I wasn't the most athletic kid ever, but I tried to be. When I realized that blame was being put on me if my team lost, I started straying away from team sports. I started competitive golf during my freshman year of high school. I had that awkward half-softball-half-golf swing and my coach ended up saying, "whatever works." I quickly fell in love with the sport and improved my game tremendously into my sophomore year.

I ended up qualifying for the state tournament the next three years and ended up placing in the top 20 my senior year. I had no intentions of becoming a collegiate athlete until a letter came from the head golf coach at Ottawa. Needless to say, I was surprised and instantly, the path leading to the future had diverged. Do I continue to go to the college I had been planning on attending or do I give Ottawa a chance? A few weeks after that letter arrived, I attended the campus and immediately felt welcomed by the coach. He was inclusive and social and it made me feel at home. I met one of the girls on the tour too, and she also made me feel welcomed. During their golf season, I had attended a tournament in Broken Arrow where I had the opportunity to meet more of the girls and talk to the coach again. I instantly felt connected to the team and knew that coming to Ottawa University was the right decision for me.

On my visit to Ottawa University, my parents and I took a drive around the town. Something about it felt vaguely familiar. As my family and I were cruising, I finally put my finger on it: It was home. I come from a very small town in the very southeast corner of Kanas. With a population of a little over 3,000, my hometown is filled with small antique shops and locally-owned restaurants that are packed every Sunday afternoon when church lets out. A good thing about my hometown is that it was fairly close to Pittsburg, Kansas. When I seemed to compare Pittsburg and Ottawa to each other, they were practically the same; mid-sized with a university and historic sites to attract tourists. I chose Ottawa University because it did not take a big adjustment from my hometown and it felt familiar. I was right at home.

I would not have come to Ottawa University if they did not have a biology undergraduate program. I have been in love with science since I can remember and I could not see myself doing anything else besides a job in the STEM field. Growing up, my family wanted me to explore different parts and cultures of the world. We generally traveled to the Caribbean and once there, I got to experience time with marine wildlife. I fell in love with the idea of working with these kinds of animals and decided that was the career path I wanted.

When I graduate from Ottawa, my current plan is to go to graduate school at Texas A&M at Galveston and pursue my degree in marine biological studies. After finishing my schooling, I want to either work as a part of a rescue, rehabilitate, and release program or a coral restoration program. The opportunities necessary to become a marine biologist are hard to come by when you're from a small town in southeastern Kansas, but Ottawa University has a great bachelor's program that is pushing me in the right direction. At the Top Scholar's competition, I was able to talk to one of the biology professors on campus who told me that one of his students became a marine biologist, and that reassurance was even more of a reason to continue my education at Ottawa.

I am very excited to continue my degree in Ottawa's biology

program. I have already taken a few classes for the major requirements and have gained a certain connection with the teachers and my classmates that I wouldn't have received at a bigger university. I am looking forward to the knowledge I will gain and the relationships I will make along the way as I move toward my goal.

My first-semester experience at Ottawa University has been everything I wanted and more. I have met so many new people, learned about new cultures, and learned many life lessons in the short four months of the first semester. I am beyond excited to continue my academic career at Ottawa University and I'm eager to see what lies ahead of me here. There have already been plenty of up and downs, such as adjusting to college life as a student-athlete and being granted the opportunity of traveling out of the States to help others. I am proud to call Ottawa University my home.

Lindi Schmelzer is a freshman from Columbus, Kansas and is a member of the Braves women's golf team. Lindi is majoring in biology and expects to graduate in 2024. Following graduation, she plans to apply to Texas A&M at Galveston to pursue further studies in marine biology.

ALEXIS SCHULTZE

As a "townie," as a student of OU who has grown up in Ottawa, Kansas is called, Ottawa University was not where I initially thought I would choose to go to school. I took a tour of the university, and I fell in love with the beauty of the campus. I love this environment, and even being from Ottawa, I have experienced things here that I never had in my entire time of living in this town. I love the small school atmosphere Ottawa brings, and it has a sense of community. As a school with a smaller student body, I can make friends very quickly and really make a connection with a diverse group of people. I have already made lots of friends who I feel will be friends for a very long time.

Unlike most students at the university, I do not play a sport. When I first joined the university, I signed a letter of intent to play soccer, but I ended up changing my mind with the intent to just focus on my education. It was a hard adjustment for me at first to be going to university, and not be involved in some form of athletics since my entire life I had been involved in some type of sport. However, after much consideration, I decided the primary reason for me being at OU was to get an education, and I wanted to make that my top priority before I decided whether or not I could commit to a team.

At Ottawa, it is quite uncommon for a student not to be involved in a sport, as the number that I have heard for the student athlete population is around ninety-eight percent. I learned early on, even in orientation, that I would be looked upon as "different" in some situations due to my lack of involvement in a sport. I have been in classes where the teachers will tell the students, "Let's go around the room, and each of you tell the rest of the class which sport you all participate in." That has been a little uncomfortable for me at times considering I am not currently playing a sport. While there have been a few of those uncomfortable situations, I have been able to find other ways to become involved in OU campus life.

Some ways that I have been able to get involved are participating in different clubs. The club that I have been the most involved in is Chi Alpha, one of the on-campus ministries. This club meets once a week and its goal is to be "The best 60-minute study break of your week." To be honest, that has proven to be true for me. Every week when I attend the club, it is a way for me to take a breath from my studies and to really center myself spending a little time with Jesus.

Another significant thing that I have been a part of is one of the university's choirs, Vox Fortis. The ladies in the choir have been so welcoming to me. Our director is so humorous, and she really makes every class time enjoyable. As one of the only freshmen in choir, I thought it was going to be a little difficult to keep up with the other girls who had been in it for two or three years, but they turned out to be very welcoming and encouraging when I have struggled with some part of a song. Even though I'm not participating in a sport, I have found that participating in Chi Alpha, Vox Fortis, and other campus activities have helped me enjoy my freshman year college experience. I really have enjoyed what Ottawa has had to offer me in my time here thus far, and I hope to continue to get involved in the future.

Looking ahead to the remainder of my time at OU, I am hopeful that I can become even more involved in campus life. I have been involved in Chi Alpha, but I hope that eventually I can be a part of the leadership team of the club. A couple of the leaders of the club have really taken me under their wings, and I have really appreciated them looking out for me. I strive to be like them if I am given the chance to be a part of the leadership team. One of the leaders of the club is also a part of the choir and she has been there for a couple of years now. She has been very helpful with choir things and she has been one of the individuals who has taken me under their wings. She has helped me get more involved in the club, and she has really been a role model to me through this first semester of college. I really hope as my time goes on at the university that I can be like her to incoming underclassmen and can encourage them to be comfortable enough to get involved in Chi Alpha as well as other campus activities outside of sports.

Ultimately, my college experience so far has been an extremely positive one. I have really enjoyed all my time at Ottawa, from the beginning orientation to my last finals. I have stepped out of my comfort zone when it has come to getting involved in things around campus when I didn't know very many people here. My college life has been very busy with homework and trying to work a job, but it has been fun trying to balance all the different things in my life while still trying to find time to have fun and relax a little. I would not exchange what I have obtained in knowledge over this past semester for anything. I have learned a lot in the classroom as well as life lessons. As I go through college, one of my significant goals is to keep an open mind and daily to continue to be a student inside and outside the classroom.

Alexis Schultze is a sophomore from Ottawa, Kansas and is a member of the Vox Fortis choir. She is majoring in exercise science and philosophy, politics, and economics. She intends to graduate in 2025. Following graduation, Alexis wants to apply for ultrasound technician school or law school.

KAYLA SMOCKS

John Maxwell once said, "Life is a matter of choices and every choice you make, makes you." With that quote in mind, I knew how important choosing the best college for myself would be. It would be a place where I'd spend the next four years of this life developmental stage, growing into the person I wanted to become in the long run. I wanted to make the right choice so I wouldn't have to go through the complications of transferring or dropping out due to being somewhere that wasn't a good fit for me.

During my college-decision time frame, I was looking for a diverse university with my intended major, a decent volleyball program, and somewhere preferably close to home. I had started with a list of schools, each of which I had been accepted into but never got the chance to visit due to COVID restrictions. I didn't want to make a decision without being able to have a feel for the campus and town environment. In the last semester of my senior year, I got an email from the OU volleyball head coach asking me to come for a visit. In all honesty, I'd never even heard of Ottawa until I opened that email. Seeing that it was only an hour from home, my mother and I decided to check it out and set up a visit.

We got to Ottawa an hour early to scope out the surroundings. Coming from a big city, it was quite calming to enter the small college town of Ottawa, Kansas. After doing a little sightseeing, we came to the campus and began the visit process. When I was on a virtual conference call with the volleyball players, I found out that I actually knew someone already on the team as well as one of the assistant coaches who had reached out to me in my younger years. The girls on the team informed me about the coaching staff, practice schedules, things to do around Ottawa during free time, and the overall life of a student-athlete at the school. After that, I was led on a tour of the campus.

Our tour guide was honest about his experience, the ups and downs, and how OU had changed his life for the better. Though that was reassuring, we knew he was somewhat obligated to convince me to like the school by the end of the tour. So once the visit was complete, we stayed and walked by ourselves. We got to see some students walking around and engaging in daily activities. As we walked by the cafeteria, there was a girl sitting outside minding her own business. My mother decided to go up to her and ask about her experience since she wasn't a hired tour guide but just a regular student.

She shared her truth with us about the school's diversity, education, and extracurricular activities. Only good things were said even when we asked about the faults she simply stated, "Well, it's still school and there are classes." Being able to easily engage and connect with this person allowed me to get insight into what it would be like to attend OU and I loved that. I left the campus thinking there was a 99.9% chance I would attend. A few weeks later, I competed for the Top Scholar program and was awarded the highest achievement. This sealed the deal, leaving me with 100% assurance that I'd be attending Ottawa for the next four years. I was lucky enough to get into a school with great academics, amazing people, and an uplifting community that truly wanted to see me succeed. That is why I chose Ottawa University

When it comes to college, there is so much to look forward to. I'm mostly looking forward to growing my knowledge in my field while gaining connections and confidence through my experience at Ottawa. From a young age, I always knew I wanted to do something in the medical field. As I continued to grow, play various sports, and witness injuries of my friends, I found a passion to help athletes get back to the activities they enjoyed. I've had my major picked since freshman year of high school. I picked courses and extracurriculars with connections to exercise science and enjoyed them all.

When I visited OU, an academic advisor informed me that my major, exercise science, was the most popular one at the University so I'd be surrounded by people on a similar path as I was on. I was pretty happy to find this out. I knew that with it being the most popular major, it would help me find more of a competitive drive to excel. Also, there would be so many resources for me to use, which was quite a relief. I would be around someone with the same major as I had almost everywhere I turned. Each of these factors would help me become more confident in my learning while also creating bonds that will be helpful in the future. As a current student, I can confidently say it's fun to be surrounded by people who want to succeed. I feel that at Ottawa, everyone has that drive to succeed in either their sports, academics, or both.

Along with making connections, I'm excited to see how I grow as a person and companion to others. I know there will be days or even weeks where I won't want to go to classes, workouts or practices, just wanting to hang out with friends and party on weekends. I want to see myself finally learn time management so when I get a job, I won't have to worry about bad habits. I feel as though college is that time period when you truly form into yourself. The standards and rules have been set for the past 18 years, and college is somewhat like an ultimate life test where you use everything you've learned to start your adulthood on the right or wrong path.

Kayla Smocks is a freshman from Kansas City, Missouri and is a member of the Braves volleyball team. Kayla is majoring in exercise science and expects to graduate in 2025. Following graduation, Kayla plans to attend graduate school to pursue her doctorate degree.

MEADOW STULL

The search to find the right school was very hard and full of challenges. COVID made it difficult to view dorms or talk to very many professors. One thing that stood out to me about Ottawa University was its Top Scholar's program. In high school, I always worked very hard to be at the top of my class, working with other students whose goals were the same. The Top Scholar's program also holds us to high expectations such as having a 3.0 GPA and being active in our community and school.

Another reason Ottawa University stood out to me so much was its softball program. In 2021, they were KCAC champions and also went to Georgia and competed for a national championship. Throughout this season so far, I have made amazing friends and have grown as a player. When I was a young girl, softball was always my passion. Ottawa University has helped me reach my softball goals and dreams. Softball has given me a family while I am at school and the sisters I've never had.

One of the most important reasons I chose Ottawa was its location. I have grandparents who live in Ottawa and my hometown of Paola, Kansas is only 30 minutes away. This gave me the option to go home if I was having a bad day or wanted to see my family, and also gave me a place to do laundry. I have a younger brother who is nine years old and I am very close to him. I want to be able to go to his basketball and soccer games and any other school events that he may have, although I have learned that staying at school over the weekend is very beneficial. I love going home and seeing my family, but I also love the relationships I have made in school.

Although I wanted to choose a school that was close to home, I didn't want to go to one with any of my high school friends. I wanted to branch out and make new relationships. I am glad I did, for if I had gone to school with some of my friends, I wouldn't have made the friendships that I have now. I have met people from different states and countries they are some of my best friends

Ottawa University's campus size and faculty ratio also had a big impact on my school-finding journey. Coming from a small high, I never wanted to go to a big college. I liked the idea of my professors and I knowing each other. I know if I have a problem with one of my classes, I can go in and ask a professor who will help, no matter what the question is. Also, with coming to a small campus are the many activities and benefits such as axe throwing, donut runs, and foam parties during orientation.

The dorms and meal plans were also very influential when I was choosing a school. Ottawa University has dorms that are suite style, which means we still have three other roommates but we only share a bathroom with those three people. This was appealing to me rather than the traditional dorm style, although Ottawa University does have both traditional and suite-style dorms. The location of the dorms is also very nice. I never have to walk more than five minutes to any of my classes. This is nice when the weather is super cold or hot. We are also very close to the cafeteria where we can eat whatever we want with our unlimited meal plans. We also have a Starbucks in the cafe which is great right before a morning class. Ottawa's meal plan was better than any other school I had visited. The quality of the food is also exceptional.

My spirituality was a big factor in choosing my school. Ottawa University is a Baptist school. I am a Presbyterian Christian and although they are not the same, they are very similar. I like the idea of being able to talk about religion in class and having professors who have the same beliefs as I. I knew there were also going to be clubs such as Chi Alpha and FCA. Chi Alpha has been one of the best things that I have come across this year. We meet every Wednesday and share our faith and sing together. It is definitely one of the best parts of my week. I have only been at Ottawa University for one semester but I have grown so much in my faith.

One of the last reasons I chose Ottawa University was its art program. I want to be an art teacher. I have met many teachers who have come from Ottawa University. They are some of the best teachers I have ever met. I was able to see the art program before committing to OU. When I saw it, I was amazed by the work that the students were creating. I want to grow as an artist and I felt that Ottawa University would be the best place for me. I knew that I wouldn't be in an art room with 100 other students, but rather would be in a small room and have one-on-one time with my teacher if needed.

Over the next four years, I am looking forward to many things. The thing that most excites me is growing as a Christian, softball player, and person. I feel as though I have grown so much already and I've only been here for one year. I love that Ottawa has given me so much room to grow and be my own person. I have learned so much from my peers and professors already. I can't wait to see what else is in store.

Overall, I am extremely pleased that I chose Ottawa University. There is no other school that is even close to Ottawa. The school and the town, in general, are amazing. Downtown Ottawa is so beautiful and filled with kind and loving people. When I came on my visit, I was greeted with smiles and kind souls. I wouldn't want to be anywhere else for the amazing journey that college is.

Meadow Stull is a freshman from Paola, Kansas and is a member of the Braves softball team. She is majoring in elementary education and art education and expects to graduate in 2025. Following graduation, Meadow plans to pursue a teaching career.

JULIA WALTMAN

Choosing a college is not an easy decision for high school students to make. It is a decision that should be made taking into account many serious considerations. Some of the factors that go into the choice are the size of the town/campus, the diversity of the school, the faculty/staff members who represent the university, and the majors offered and they are all important to varying degrees. A college campus will be a student's home-away-from-home for the next four years, so being comfortable at their university is very important. Below are some of the reasons that led me to choose Ottawa University as the place to call my home for the next four years.

One of the main reasons I chose to attend Ottawa was the atmosphere of the town and the campus. Coming from a smaller community in Oklahoma, I wanted to feel the same as I would at home, which was a smaller community with access to larger communities if needed. Ottawa is the perfect fit for me because the town has that small-town feel, but one can easily access larger cities like Kansas City, Lawrence, or Overland Park for other needs. The OU campus also has that at-home feeling. The campus is not spread out over a large area so getting around campus is more accessible and enjoyable.

Not only is the campus smaller, but so are the classes. My classes at Ottawa have been small, which allows the professors to get to know each of the students and help their students out when needed. I came from a smaller school in Oklahoma, so when I was told that Ottawa University was a smaller university, I was intrigued. The class sizes are smaller than my high school classes, so it was nice to get a college professor's undivided attention when needed. With over 90% of the school being athletes, the teachers understand the late nights and missing classes for the activity, and they are willing to work with us to make sure we do not get behind in the class.

Another reason I chose Ottawa University was the diversity of the school. With over 30 sports available for men and women plus multiple clubs available, OU has a wide variety of diverse students to interact with. I feel this is an essential aspect as I grow into an adult. The diverse cultural and ethnic backgrounds from all over the world are on display at Ottawa. It is fun and exciting to learn and interact with other students from different backgrounds and cultures. My living arrangement also displays the diversity of Ottawa University. My dorm is an eight-person dorm, and it consists of girls from different sports other than softball who are also from various ethnic backgrounds. That is very important to me because I am able to interact with these girls daily. This will allow us to grow as individuals and learn to respect others and their differences.

The coaches, faculty, and staff are crucial to any university. You can get a good indication of how campus life is by how they treat others while representing the university off-campus. My first interaction with anyone from Ottawa University was with the assistant softball coach, Sam Mendez. I could tell by the way she treated me and talked about Ottawa University that it was a unique university. While on my first visit, I met with head softball coach Jay Kahnt and received the same type of treatment from him as well, not only towards myself but also towards my family. From that moment on, I knew I would end up calling Ottawa home! The coaches were always upfront and honest with me about the process, and I never felt like just a number to them. I always have the feeling of family when talking with the coaches.

But it does not stop with the coaches; the softball team was there to help me during my recruitment. I got to eat and talk to them about the team and how the coaches were during on and off-field activities. We also talked about the school and all the classes and majors available. I felt comfortable talking with all the girls, and they were very welcoming toward me. When it came to move-in day, the softball team met me at my dorm and helped me move stuff in, and made me feel at home. I genuinely feel I have made numerous lifetime friends already. These actions speak volumes about the culture that has been created at Ottawa University, and I will always be grateful to be a part of that culture.

Ottawa has more than 50 different majors available to students. One of Ottawa's most popular majors, which is mine also, is exercise science. It means many of my teammates and roommates are in some of my classes or have already taken those classes. Having my teammates in those classes makes it more manageable to form study groups to help when we are away from classes for activities or to help prepare for finals.

Deciding what college to attend was not an easy decision and there were many factors that I had to consider when choosing the best college for me. I feel I have made the perfect decision not only for my softball career but also for my personal development. Over the past couple of months, I have been very proud to call Ottawa my home. There are many activities in town and the community is very welcoming to the students. The town/community has made me feel at home.

Additionally, the size of the campus is perfect for me, and I am excited about my future at Ottawa University. The faculty and staff at school are very helpful and polite. Everyone on campus would go out of their way to help me or anyone else when needed. As for the softball team, they have become my second family and we treat each other as such. I love how the small class sizes have helped me learn more and the teachers are there for me any time I need help.

Finally, I have also had the privilege of meeting many people from all over the world and I am lucky that I got to meet them. I have learned more about where they are from and their cultures, but more importantly, I'm thrilled to call them my friends. I am very proud to call Ottawa my second home.

Julia Waltman is a freshman from Harrah, Oklahoma and is a member of the Braves softball team. Julia is majoring in exercise science and expects to graduate in 2025. Following graduation, Julia plans to apply to MLB teams to become an athletic trainer for professional baseball players.

DARBY WEIDL

Growing up in Ottawa, I always heard about the university and was introduced to the campus, students, and events when I was young. During elementary school, we would annually attend events that would be held on campus. This included an author fair, track meets, Christmas programs, and many other inclusive events. During middle school, many Ottawa University students would come to the school, work with students in classes, and get student-teaching experience. The college students' attendance in the classroom made the middle schoolers eager to learn more about the University and gave the students a role model. In high school, there were multiple games or meets where Ottawa University coaches would be sitting in the crowd supporting the team and recruiting. Sometimes they would even bring their team to support.

I wasn't sure if I would still have the feeling of going to college and that's why I was hesitant to attend. However, being on campus and meeting other students have proven me wrong. I have met amazing roommates who have made my first semester incredible, and students who I now call friends in my classes. I now know that I get the full college experience at Ottawa University and I encourage other students who grew up in Ottawa not to overlook it.

My parents are alumni of Ottawa University and it is where they met and received their education. My mom also grew up in Ottawa and went to a different institution for a year when she decided she wanted to attend Ottawa University for one year. So when making my decision to continue my academics at OU, it was almost like following in her footsteps. My dad, on the other hand, attended Ottawa University on a football scholarship for two-and-a-half years and then received his bachelors in human services. They both had many great experiences and stories to tell about Ottawa University, and knowing it is their alma mater makes the university that more special to me.

When choosing where to spend the next four years of my life, a lot of factors were in play when making my decision. A few of the steps I took when choosing Ottawa University included seeing how their offered majors fit into my desired degree, the athletics, and most importantly, the culture. All these things are important to me because college isn't just preparing you for what I may want my career to be, but it's preparing me for the real world and a new journey I'm going to be on.

Growing up, I always had an interest in working with children and I have always valued helping others. As I began to branch out and take different classes in high school, I found a love while working in the CTE program where I made lesson plans and taught pre-schoolers. While taking those classes, I also found a passion for science and the anatomy of the human body. This led me to learning more about the job of a pediatrician and the medical work they do with children every day. These high school class experiences led me to start looking for good collegiate science programs to continue my education and discovered that Ottawa's biology and exercise science programs are phenomenal.

In the classroom, the professors are very hands-on and interactive. Questions are encouraged and the environment makes me eager to learn. The labs each week are interactive and push me to step outside my comfort zone. The best part is how the professors value strong student-teacher relationships. This helps develop respect for one another and makes me excited to attend their class.

Ottawa University, while known for their academic excellence, also excels in their athletics and offers more than 30 different teams. While I was in the recruiting process, the coaches for both volleyball and women's wrestling treated me with nothing but respect and were sure to value both the importance of academics and athletics. I especially enjoyed learning about SALT, a club that promotes student-athletes supporting other student-athletes.

Growing up, I attended many volleyball camps and did many lessons with Head Coach Blessington which introduced me to and made me comfortable with the volleyball program early on. I initially only wanted to play volleyball in college and had planned to attend a different institution. But my plans changed when over the summer I decided I was not ready to end my career of women's wrestling. I talked to both the wrestling and volleyball coaches quite a bit and we managed to balance my schedule so I can do both sports.

Becoming a part of the program here was a blessing, giving me the opportunity to continue my volleyball career while wrestling. The focus that is given to every individual athlete in the gym during practice is something that I really value about the volleyball program. The large number in the program is an opportunity other volleyball programs do not have and allows us to experience different scrimmages, looks, and scenarios within practices. The volleyball program is a team like I've never been a part of and made my first semester an amazing experience.

With women's wrestling being so new to society and beginning to grow, I knew I wanted to be a part of that. It just so happened that my high school coach, Dalton Weidl, had taken a job at Ottawa University to be the head coach of women's wrestling. Coach Weidl is also my older brother, and he began coaching me in my junior year when I first started wrestling. He and I work well together in the practice room, bouncing ideas back and forth and discussing how the workload is as a student-athlete, and I believe our relationship also helps him with his relationships with other athletes. Because Dalton and I have always been close, I think that it translates into my seeing my teammates as my family as well. If you ask any of my teammates, my brother is not just a coach to us, he is a friend and leader, but most importantly, it's what makes us a family.

Coach Weidl is working to build a strong women's wrestling program and when he explained the plan he has for the program, I knew that I could help play a part. Growing up, we were taught hard work, dedication, and a little bit of fun are what it takes to achieve our goals. That is exactly what we do in the women's wrestling program at OU. All of us are skilled wrestlers who love the sport and value a good work ethic and a positive attitude. The focus of changing the culture and building rock-solid programs is not what sets just the women's wrestling program apart from any other university, but it is what sets *all* athletics at Ottawa University apart.

Ottawa University is a community in itself and that is what makes it so special to me. There are many programs and clubs that incorporate the Ottawa community and keep the town involved with the university. Ottawa University works to construct a contagious environment and culture of support and encouragement that helps students confidently adventure down any path they choose, and I am proud to be a part of this community for the next four years.

Darby Weidl is a freshman from Ottawa, Kansas and is a member of the Braves volleyball and women's wrestling team. She also participates in student council and SALT. Darby is majoring in biology and expects to graduate in 2025. Following graduation, Darby plans to attend medical school.

ADDISON ZURCHER

Why Ottawa University? In fact, why any university? They are hard questions to answer, yet they are questions every single person who decides to attend college must answer. For me, I had a list of mandatory requirements I wanted the institution I attend to possess. I wanted an environment that was more personal; smaller class-to-professor ratio, a total population which promoted more opportunities for one-on-one interactions, a place where I knew any opportunities I wanted to be part of would not fill up, and a place that accepted student-athletes with open arms.

I came from a small high school an hour outside of Kansas City, Missouri. I had always grown up with small class sizes, which allowed me to really connect with my teachers. I always had the ability and felt comfortable asking questions in class and talking to my teachers one on one for extra help. This really helped me with my academic success, so when looking for colleges, I needed a school that was also able to provide me with the same opportunities in the classroom. Ottawa is exceptional when it comes to class sizes and making sure professors are able to personalize classes and lectures to those in the class.

Another thing Ottawa is able to provide which impressed me was the tutors. If you are struggling with any classes and need a little help, there are tutors for every subject/class. The nice thing about tutoring at OU is the tutors have all taken the classes they tutor so they can provide an understanding of professors and how they teach as well as help on understanding the material. Students normally get their tutor's number so they don't have to go through a secondary source to get in contact with them.

Since Ottawa University is such a small school, we don't have to worry about getting into the classes we want. As long as we sign up for classes in the scheduled time, it is very easy to get placed into the courses we need or want without having to fight for a spot or being waitlisted. I will never miss out on an amazing opportunity at Ottawa because the experience there is so personalized. Our course advisors are just a phone call away, and we are able to meet them during the week, call them or email them and get prompt responses with any questions we have on enrollment or schedule conflicts. No one falls through the cracks here.

As a student-athlete, I have always had to be able to balance a busy schedule. Coming to a school that had many sports and consequently many student-athletes, I have found so much support. Coaches understand you're a student before you're an athlete and promote studying and spending time on school work. The professors are understanding of a missed class due to a sporting event and are willing to assist you with missed course work and readings. They are very flexible and willing to accommodate you and help give you alternative times to do labs, lectures, tests, etc. This was quite attractive to me signing on to be a student-athlete for OU. Where I have a love for my sport, I know my academics are what will build my foundation for my future. The coaches and faculty understand the importance of supporting student-athletes in their academic and athletic success.

Being a predominantly sports-oriented school also offers another perk. Because there are so many sports offered at the university, coaches recruit for each sport all over the country and world. Just on my team alone, we have girls from Iceland, Sweden, Brazil, Ireland, and the Netherlands. I have loved getting to meet girls from all around the world, learning their cultures, and seeing how training and play differs in their countries. I have become close with several of the girls and have really enjoyed showing them some of the fun things that rural America has to offer.

The community of Ottawa, Kansas was another strong component for choosing to say yes to OU. In a small town like Ottawa, we get so much support, not just from fellow students, alumni, and staff, but also from the families who live around the college. The restaurants have OU flags and are always supporting our game-time information for the townspeople to be in the know. Families attend our games. It is fun to see little leagues attend games and watch them dream of one day being on the field. The small town also has many amenities that allow us as athletes and students to have fun and unwind. There are plenty of places to eat if you need a break from the cafeteria, there is a hospital for any sports injuries or illness that might arise, and there are a ton of mom-and-pop restaurants from pizza to diners that let you feel like you are home.

School community also plays a huge role in choosing to

come to OU. Staff are willing to help you find resources and the janitorial staff in the dorms go out of their way to help you with anything you need. Students help each other out. It's so nice to see when a soccer game is going on the lacrosse teams come to cheer them on and vice versa. Every sport on campus supports the other teams. Coming to a school of Ottawa's size, we get to truly know the people around us. It's a great feeling and place to be. I can truly say Ottawa is a home away from home.

I'm most excited to continue to experience all the fun activities the school hosts, and to grow closer to more people at the school. Ottawa has a wide variety of people from different areas, states, and different countries. You get to meet people from all over the world and are able to learn so much from each other. It's not at every school you have the ability to talk to people from Italy, Ireland, and other countries, go to class with each other, and play on the same field or court together. Ottawa is a great place to be. I'm so happy I chose to attend this university and am excited to see what else they have to offer as I continue my schooling here.

Addison Zurcher is a freshman from Pleasant Hill, Missouri. She is a member of the Braves women's soccer team. Addison is a biology major and plans to graduate in the spring of 2025. Following graduation, Addison plans to attend medical school and pursue a career as a family physician.

SECTION TWO

Second-year scholars reflected on their personal journey at Ottawa thus far, and answered: "How have you changed during your time at Ottawa? What advice would you give to your first-year-self, if you could send yourself a brief note?"

In their second year, our scholars are coming into their own. Having for the most part found their bearings and taken full control of the wheel, they are now setting the course for the rest of their college careers and beyond. These students are in a very exciting time in their lives, and it is both fun and heartwarming to hear about their own perception of this moment in their lives. These students have grown and transformed, and their introspective efforts are impressive and inspiringly optimistic.

HANNAH DEWARE

Besides the obvious "another year older and another year wiser," I have grown exponentially since the last time I sat down to write for the Scholar's book. In the name of stating the obvious, I've received another year of higher education and another year of experience in this weird, wild world we call society; this, which is less obvious, means that I have more independence to thrive, more critical thinking skills to comprehend, more viewpoints to account for, more meanings to understand, more . . . of *everything* to grapple with. What once seemed as easy as two plus two now feels like solving an unsolvable trigonometry proof, the context of which has much more complex ideas and thoughts for me to reckon with. Understanding the world I am now coming to see is more difficult than rocket science and I would know. I can do rocket science. But, oddly enough, I cannot comprehend the *literal meaning of life,* or in more serious terms, communication between other people (fitting the bill of a nerd struggling with social interaction, I know).

What used to be a naive look at a simplistic world I *survived in* has now become a critical point of view on the intricate messy society *that I now live in.* Notice that word choice: *survive* versus *live.* Sure, my old view was definitely easy but it was simply only that: easily digestible. I now know that understanding our world we now find ourselves in is anything but digestible. It is something that I, and millions of other people, choke on and struggle to swallow because of the greasy and sour taste of the shockingly grim reality of 2021.

Frightfully corrupt politics, unnerving racist propaganda, and terrifying acts of unnoticed injustice plague our humanity and infect our society. All this is not even to mention the actual plague of Covid-19 which has dramatically infected and changed the world forever. But I now *live* because I now see the disgusting parts. Put more simply, I can see the dark but only if I also see the light too — new representation in government, advocacy for change, beautiful works of kindness and love between humanity. Nothing about the world is easy nor would I ever want it to be. Somewhere in this mess of grossness and gorgeousness I fit in, and I would much rather see the world for what it is than survive in ignorance.

Now, my dear reader, is where I offer a soft trigger warning as I write about one of the biggest factors that forced me to change and then subsequently grow this past year. Eighty-one percent of women have experienced sexual harassment in their lifetime, especially those between the ages of eighteen to twenty-five, as reported by NPR on February of 2018. Sadly, I am not a part of the nineteen percent that goes unscathed because in the last year I reported sexual harassment that had been happening to me. The following six months was a rollercoaster of emotions and hardships, to say the very least.

My naive view of the world shattered on the cold floor of an early January morning as I witnessed and experienced firsthand some of those cruel acts of humanity, the people who called me a liar, the people who I thought were friends who turned out not to be, the people who ridiculed me for not saying something sooner. I was terrified of leaving my dorm room. I was terrified of myself even. But there is a knight in shining armor in this not-so-fairytale of a story.

My parents became my biggest supporters when I didn't know what to do next and my best friend became my biggest advocate when I didn't have the voice to say what I needed to. Ottawa University also became a safe haven of sorts. The school had and still has resources, like Title Nine and campus counselors who are available to me in case of scenarios like mine. Without the aid of the community I had created in my first year, the quarter-life crisis I had experienced could have put a full stop to my educational journey; but it didn't stop me because I had that support of the community surrounding me.

Oh boy, that was heavy. If you've stuck with me this far, thank you and I promise that this next half of my essay won't be nearly as weighty. I pinky swear.

Last year, almost to the day I write, I joined the forensics and debate team. This was because I had recently stopped playing soccer since I was coming to discover that just because I enjoyed an activity in high school didn't mean I enjoyed it, or enjoyed it nearly as much, in college. This crossover was, to me, one of the first event signs that I was changing and therefore refining my activity taste. I more or less accidentally stumbled across the debate team as I was only looking to participate in the forensics side of things. For my dearest readers who don't know exactly what I mean by forensics, let me briefly explain.

Forensics is still a form of debate but only much softer and more personal. I am still presenting an argument but instead of the stereotypical formal debate one might expect, forensics presents arguments through personal experience of other people (think like competitive poetry or prose readings and you will get close to the idea). But back to my point, I had intended only to participate in the softer, personal side of the activity. However, in order to compete, I also had to formally debate, which, mind you, was something I had never done before. Yet through the love of forensics, and for the sake of further refining my activity taste, I undertook the task of learning formal debate and all the jargon and mess it brings.

Surprisingly I was pretty good at it. After less than half a semester of training, I argued my way to third place at nationals. Debate forced my worldview to widen, and to take in options and aspects I wouldn't have ever accounted for or realized before. Along the way, I've met people who have done the same, ones who challenge me to critically think and ones who demonstrate the real meaning of acceptance. I now am a much more well-rounded person because of forensics and debate, and they have caused me to experience the world much more realistically.

I also took up music, yet again. You see, music has always been woven into my life since the ripe old age of five when my mother put me in piano lessons, which I continued until near the end of high school. With all of the sharp edges of the world more blatant than ever, music helps me remain grounded and optimistic. I am currently in Ottawa University's concert and pep bands, both of which bring me a lot of joy. Our band is small in numbers and sometimes struggles to pull it all together, but the masterpieces we create are ones made up of many different backgrounds. Everyone in the band learned to play differently, on different instruments, in different parts of the country. Through early entrances, wrong notes, and out-of-tune pitches, we still construct a piece of art that is representative of all of us — despite how contrasting each of our playing styles are. Band and music taught me, and are still teaching me, that despite our differences, we all make *beautiful music together*. There is meaning behind everything; we simply must know where to look.

As I now draw my essay to a close, I'm not quite sure what I would tell my first-year self. There's a lot of pain and hardships that you are going to endure. You are going to lose a lot of friends and lose part of yourself, too. You're going to learn that life will kick you hard, in the face even, and wait for you to get back up just so it can kick you in the shins. But each time you fall, you get back up stronger, with stronger friendships and a stronger sense of self. You will grow and adapt and change. You will grapple with *everything*. I guess if I had to tell my younger self something, it would go like this:

Dearest me,

Learn to live, because it feels much better than surviving. Not everyone is who they say they are, but don't be scared to find your people. Try new things, yet don't forget the old ones either. And above all, the meaning of life might be harder than rocket science, but if anyone can figure it out, it is definitely you.

Hannah Deware is a sophomore from Atchison, Kansas. She is a member of the debate and forensics team, wind ensemble, and pep band. Hannah is majoring in communications and secondary education in English, as well as pursuing theater education. She expects to graduate the in 2024. Her post-graduate plans include becoming a teacher while working to achieve a master's degree.

KARLEY FAUDERE

Change is one of the inevitable and often annoyingly un-avoidable parts of life. However, lately as I have looked in the mirror and stopped to listen to myself speak, that inevitable change is not so annoying. The growth I have personally experienced in a mere year of college is a source of great pride for me. Not only am I a better student with more knowledge, but I am also a stronger, wiser, more productive human being. My time at Ottawa has begun to change me in numerous ways, both in the classroom and in things that extend far beyond my work in the classroom.

For my entire life, I have been a driven student, a devoted athlete, and an independent human being. As I have progressed over the last year and a half, I have found myself to be even more driven, devoted, and independent. It is often the case that the value of being on your own two feet and learning your own way are under appreciated. However, now I believe independence to be instrumental in teaching anyone who they are and who they aspire to be.

A year ago, I was wide eyed with ten million aspirations in life but have since found myself absorbed in a few passions rather than a feeble attempt at being the jack of all trades. To myself I would have said, as the saying goes, "find your passion and become a master of it." I am sure that a year from today my passions will have evolved even more, and to my future self I say the same thing: "Work to become what fills your soul. Work to become what gives you purpose. Work to become what makes you happy. This life is long and it would be quite the blessing to spend it loving who you are becoming but this life is also fast-paced and disappears before you know it." What a shame it would be to not spend this life as the very best version of myself.

During my time at Ottawa, I have been without adult supervision for the first time in my life and I have learned that I am unbelievably independent. No obstacle has been too large for me to conquer when I put my mind to doing so. I have learned that I am capable of so much more than I thought I was. Without a hand to hold every day, I have excelled at the commitments I have made to academics, athletics, and myself. I am stronger than I was before Ottawa. I am more resilient in every aspect of my life.

My independence, however, has taught me balance. Balance has become important in my everyday success. I have had to decide what few things are most important to me so that I can succeed at those without anyone's help. Independence removes extra working hands in my life, but it also teaches me the value of the two hands attached to the end of my own arms. My expectations for myself have neither plateaued nor have they decreased in the past year. I have successfully raised my expectations for myself in life and continue to find ways to meet those new expectations.

In high school I would pass my classes with flying colors but I never really learned the material, I memorized it. I set a new expectation for myself to pass with those same flying colors but to absorb every bit of knowledge I could in my college courses, and I have found that my curiosity to learn is increasing daily after setting that expectation for myself. I also aspired to be a better athlete and to push my limits on the court and in the gym. This has also been a successful endeavor of my independence. I am stronger, faster, and more competitive as a result of my own efforts.

College is difficult and pushes us intellectually and socially to find a place in the world. Though I am not entirely sure that I have quite found that place, I am also entirely sure that I will. Each and every day I learn more about myself in the smallest moments that seem so insignificant. I have learned that I am capable of working hard for the things I commit myself to, whether I enjoy them or not. Countless evenings spent hunched over organic chemistry books, basketball sprints at five in the morning, and long nights working can all attest to this fact.

This capability to pour my every effort into my commitments has taught me that I am a woman of her word, that I am a woman who does not live by a lukewarm effort, because giving my all to everything I do has never failed to profit me in the long run. This attribute is one I have admired in others and am pleased to see reflected in my own being. Of all the growth I expected to see in myself as I left for college, this is my favorite surprise. I believe that my resilience will serve me for as long as I live and in every small and large thing I do.

Passion is yet another attribute I have learned lives within me. I have found a passion for music not only through my violin as a musician, but also through my ears as a consumer. Music has kept me sane when I am four hours into studying and struggling to uncross my tired eyes or when I am three miles into a difficult workout. I have found a passion for science and the evidence that gives it validity. As a science major and aspiring doctor I should be so lucky as to have a pure love for studying, exploring, and learning what will be my lifelong craft.

I have also found a passion for art and the way that it depicts the world in such a soothing way. Art displays the passions of an individual and is a welcomed reflection of my own passions on my social media, my phone, and the walls of my room. Art has allowed me to surround myself with reminders and emblems of the things I love.

I have found a passion for education, and the joy that comes from new understanding. Until my last day on this earth, I hope to love learning, because learning has enriched me as a person in unexpected ways. I am more aware of the cultures of others, of the beliefs of the world, and of the science of humans, animals, and plants, and I am all the richer for it. I have found a passion for nutrition and how it affects my longevity and day-to-day functions. I like to feel good, I mean, who doesn't? A better understanding of nutrition has given me an awareness of what makes me feel good and of what makes me a better student athlete.

Last, I have found a passion for faith. Most of who I am and what I do stems from what I believe. My faith has grown tremendously as I have had the opportunity to understand what it means to me when no one else is looking. My faith has grown as I have been away from my parents and had the opportunity to see my faith in action without wondering if it was merely because my parents believed in God and therefore, blindly, so did I. My faith is the cornerstone of every passion I have and of every action I take.

My hair is longer, I eat differently, I am now allergic to new things, I have a high school diploma, I am more traveled, I am a half an inch taller, I live in a different small town in Kansas, and I truly enjoy tea now, but I suppose looking back, little has changed about who I am during my time at Ottawa. Yes, I look different and minor bits of me have evolved but who I am day in and day out is fundamentally the same. I have not changed rather I have learned who I am along the way.

I have learned just how passionate I am about music,

science, art, education, nutrition, and faith. I have learned that I am capable of enduring work that may not put a smile on my face but benefits me in the long run. I have learned that I am an independent woman who actively chooses to better herself and her world. I cannot speak much of the change that Ottawa has sparked in me, but I value the person it has taught me that I am. If I could speak to my younger me, if I could change anything . . . well, I wouldn't. I would simply let her endure all of the same battles, all of the same challenges, and all of the independence that has made the person writing this paper today. I am proud of who I am now and excited for who I will be tomorrow. Change may not be the correct word for my time at Ottawa, but realization certainly is.

Karley Faudere is a sophomore from El Dorado, Kansas. She is a member of the women's basketball team, track team, and is also a resident assistant. Karley is majoring in biology and expects to graduate in 2024. Following graduation, Karley plans to apply to a doctoral program and pursue medical genetics.

JONATHAN FOX

When I first came into Ottawa University, I had little-to-no expectations. All I knew was that I was about to be away from home for one of the first times. Ottawa is only twenty minutes away from home, but it was still a new feeling. I moved into Bennet Hall and was already too scared to have a real conversation with my roommates and therefore spent almost the entire first week in my bedroom, except for football, classes, and mealtimes. I slowly started to come out of my shell and would talk to my roommates and get to know them a little better. I would eventually start talking to random people around campus and on the football team. I made some really good friends when I eventually came out of my shell and decided not to be a scared little freshman anymore.

The decision to actually go out and talk to people was easily one of the best decisions I have made at Ottawa simply because then I had people to talk to about the struggles of being a first-gen college student. I had people to study with and go out and have fun with. I started out as a scared little freshman and now I am a resident assistant. The job forces me to be more social than most students on campus and I love it. Being an RA gives me a chance to go out and push those students who were just like me.

I also became an orientation leader in hopes of helping incoming freshmen and discouraging them from staying in their room because I had learned from personal experience that Ottawa is entirely what you make of it. Whatever walk of life you come from, you will more than likely find others that are the same way. Ottawa conforms to every students' wants and needs as best as a small college can. Every year, the college has comment boxes for students to say what changes they would like to see on campus. The student government also makes big decisions throughout the school year based on what the students want.

I came into Ottawa wanting some kind of business degree, but didn't know exactly what I wanted to do. So, I took some business classes and chose business economics, which was good for a little bit, but I didn't really feel like I was getting into it, so I switched over to accounting because it made more sense to me. Ottawa always has me switching gears, and always puts me just outside my comfort zone, enough to find something else that I might find interesting. This taught me to be comfortable being outside of my comfort zone.

In high school, I never really had to study and rarely left school with the homework assigned because I could do it in the last period of the day. In college, that changed drastically because of the lack of free time. I always struggle a little trying to figure out a rhythm at the beginning of the semester, but gradually throughout the semester, I figure it out and start to find those little gaps in my day for quick power naps, to do some homework, or for a quick game of Call of Duty.

Between sports, classes, and being an RA, I felt as if I was expected in three different places at all times. Whether it is a weight-lifting session for football at 5:45 a.m. or desk shifts in the dorms until 3:30 a.m., I'm always doing something. Back in high school, I would have time to play video games every night along with some family time, but now if I actually don't have anything to do, I feel like I need to do something. For example, for awhile on Saturday after the football season ended, I couldn't sleep in because my body still thought that it was gameday. Ottawa taught me to enjoy the time off but also how to be grateful to be busy.

When I came into my first morning football conditioning, I was incredibly out of shape, to the point where I was certain that the warm up was the workout. The coaches decided that I would make a good offensive lineman even though I had barely played any of that during my high school football career. I didn't really care where they put me because I was glad I was still playing college football. I struggled to get any kind of footwork down and couldn't block anyone. Talking to some of the coaches now, they were not sure if I was going to make it or not. Looking back at that now is funny, for I am not yet good enough to start, but I am good enough to confidently hold a spot on the team. In football, Ottawa taught me hard work pays off and changed how I look at the sport entirely.

Ottawa has taught me many things from just playing footwork for football to how to go out and talk to people. It taught me how to come out of my shell and enjoy being on campus and hanging out with friends. I have changed in many of the same ways that Ottawa has taught me how to. Ottawa doesn't force much of anything on to students, but instead tries to encourage students to make the best of every moment on campus. Ottawa changed my way of thinking from just wanting to stay in my room and play video games to wanting to go out and talk to people, meeting up with some friends in the café, or meeting some people I've never met before.

While my time at Ottawa has been short, it has been eventful. In football we won as many games as I did my entire high school career, which was five. Playing football at Ottawa had a lot of highs and lows, which I believe comes with any sport. Everyone has a bad practice once in a while. The part that made it tough was all those bad practices followed by a desk shift full of homework ending at 12:30, which was then followed by a 5:45 a.m. lifting session. The next day can be quite a struggle to get through classes and gets a little harder when practice rolls around and I haven't had a chance to get a nap in. But I always had to push through and make the most of the sleep I got that night.

If I could give my freshman self some advice, I would start of saying not to be afraid to get involved at Ottawa. I was so worried that I wouldn't have time to do anything other then football and classes, which is tough sometimes but is still doable — and I love it. Becoming an RA was one of the best decisions I have made in my time at Ottawa. I would also tell myself to not be afraid of meeting new people which means I need to get out of my bedroom more often. To make college life enjoyable I need to have friends to talk to, preferably some that are going through the same struggles that I am. Some of my first friends were freshmen football players who were the first in their family to go to college, exactly like me. Unfortunately, two of these friends ended up not coming back to Ottawa because they ultimately decided that college wasn't for them, which leads me to my next tip for my past self: Always put yourself first.

In my freshmen year, some stuff happened in my family that really brought me down for a little while. I found peace going to a weekly Bible study put on by one of the football players. Stuff will happen in school that can put anyone down, so don't be the person to sit back and feel bad for yourself, instead go out and find other things to do that keep your mind off of it. Once again, it comes back to having friends to reside in that you can trust.

One thing that you must understand about college regardless of whether or not you play a sport is that the grind never stops. The combination of sports, homework, and being an RA really isn't for everyone, and that's okay. What really matters in school is that you have to choose a grind that works for you. Maybe your schedule is full with classes and you can't handle a sport, which I'm sure most student athletes have thought was going to happen to them at some point in their career.

To sum up, Ottawa has changed me for the better by bringing me out of my comfort zone and changing my way of thinking. I wouldn't want to go anywhere other than Ottawa because of how great everyone has been, whether it is the staff or the students. For the most part, everyone is open to hearing my story if I'm willing to share it.

Jonathan Fox is a sophomore from Richmond, Kansas. He is a member of the Braves football team and is currently majoring in accounting. Jonathan plans to graduate in 2024 and pursue a career in his major.

YAN KEUWO

In my short time at Ottawa University, I've been allowed the opportunity to further develop myself into the person I one day hope to be. This has required me to change the way I view certain points, lose friends, make friends, and go out of my comfort zone—the list could go on and on. During this process in my last three semesters at Ottawa, due to the unique circumstances only this university could provide, I'm able to continue progressing toward being an independent young adult, capable of navigating my way through the world.

When first arriving at OU, I was almost as nervous as I was excited. I wasn't too far from home, but it was my first time truly being away from my family for an extended period of time. I did what most students do when they first get dropped off, which is stare at our room and wonder "What now?" I thought about how new friends would have to be made to fill the hole left by the ones from back home, restarting at a school as a freshman once again, and beginning to play football at a higher level than I'd ever experienced. Questions popped into my mind of whether I would be able to handle all the new stressors that were entering into my life. With these doubts, however, came self-reassurance.

While I don't remember exactly when it started, at a certain point I began having the utmost confidence in being comfortable with myself. While in high school, I regularly desired others to include me, which at times would leave me feeling like an outcast. Fear of missing out was constantly on my mind when I viewed the Snapchat stories of my friends, or when I scrolled through my feed on Instagram. Due to social media, members of all generations are constantly in competition with their peers regardless of whether they mean to be or not. Comparison is constantly the thief of joy as we continually aspire to be like or have what another person has.

As I sat staring at my screen and viewing all these events transpiring month after month, I came to the realization that being like everyone else wasn't what would lead me to be happy and live a full life. I had never been as loud or outgoing as the other kids growing up. When with my friends, I always had a great time, but

I wasn't constantly looking to leave the house and I enjoyed being alone more times than not throughout the week. For whatever reason, this led to me feeling as if something was wrong with me, since social media portrayed a much different picture of what was alluring to those around me.

Eventually I figured out that self-certainty was the first step to being content with myself. Being bothered by what others are able to do, what others had, or how another person was viewed were doing nothing but adding unnecessary stress to my life. All that is of significance to me now is what I think about myself in comparison to where I want to be. Of course I'm not completely arrogant as to be completely detached from others, but I no longer allow their differing lifestyles overwhelm me the way they once did. I still continue to attempt to advance, just at my own pace, free from judging myself, and unworried as to how my peers may go about achieving similar goals.

Ever since adopting this mindset, I've found that some of my wants from earlier in life were coming my way without much effort or strain on my behalf. I made friends not because I forcibly acted a certain way so that they would like me, but instead from me being me and allowing these new faces to intertwine their life stories with mine. It is true that I was a freshman once again, yet with these new authentic friends, I had people to share my new experiences with, even if it just meant going to the cafe for the first time. When it came to football with all my uncertainty about how I may perform when stacked against other players on the team, it wasn't until I began believing that I was given this opportunity for a reason and should take full advantage that I began feeling comfortable on the field.

Change in this stage of my life is a difficult task to achieve. It is rigorous work to truly alter a habit that has so deeply been instilled to one's psyche. If I were to talk to freshman-year me, the first piece of advice that I would give myself is to set goals in order to aid in this breaking-of-a-habit process. No matter how big or small the goal, setting landmarks for achievements that I actively plan to work towards and accomplish has been great for me mentally. Reaching these objectives has allowed me opportunities to distance myself from the burdens of my everyday life and create a sense of fulfillment when one was achieved. With the busyness of school, work, football, family, and having a social life, mental break can be hard to come by. I would advise myself to see these goals as mental escapes that can help me throughout the day.

To go along with having goals, my second piece of advice would be to have hobbies. I vividly remember sitting at times in my dorm room during my freshman year bored out of my mind with seemingly nothing to do. I would advise myself to search for hobbies in order to fill this time instead of mindlessly scrolling through social media again and again. Similar to setting goals, having hobbies leads to having an escape from the mundane dance that life can turn into at times. I used to search the internet high and low for activities to fill the time, not realizing that hobbies don't necessarily need to be out of this world or extraordinary; I just need to have a sense of willingness to learn from my end.

My third piece of advice is to enjoy the little moments in life. On a day-to-day basis not everything is going to be glamorous, so it's important to learn to enjoy as much as possible. Ever since I began trying to appreciate simple occasions, I've noticed the many celebratory instances that could easily have been overlooked. It can be something as simple as spending time with my roommate. Freshman year during winter and summer break, I realized how much I had taken those times for granted and I couldn't wait to see the special people I had been introduced to through Ottawa once again. With every passing minute, my life goal is to have no regrets and unfortunately, it can be a tiresome course of action; however, for me it makes all the more worth it.

Lastly, once again along similar lines, my fourth piece of advice to my freshman self would be to relish the opportunity I was given to play football at the college level. No matter whether it is D1, NAIA, or JUCO, only seven percent of high school football players are recruited to play at a higher level. While in high school, football had always been something I just did for fun until my senior year when I decided to take the sport much more seriously. Coming to Ottawa University and adapting to the large portion of time football had in my life was challenging and I found myself anxiously awaiting the end of the season at times. With practices, weights, film and all else that comes along with football which varies from being early in the morning, very cold, or just plain monotonous, it's easy to make light of the good moments.

While not loving the grind of football at all times, they are precious memories that I'll be able to hold on to for the rest of my life. Directly following the end of last season within two weeks I was already deeply missing the majority of the same things I used to complain about. With sports, especially one as physically demanding as football, I never really know when my last game may be. With the most recent season, I was injured for almost fifty percent of the season and all I really wanted to do was be able to participate. I didn't realize how much I would miss something I love until it was taken away from me.

In conclusion, my time at Ottawa University has allowed me the chance to take a deeper look at myself and decide what I truly want. I've learned that being patient with myself is not only extremely necessary, but also perfectly fine. There is no reason to force acting a certain way just to be able to relate to my peers. Those who accept me as I am are the only ones that I need to concern myself with. Ultimately from my freshman year until now, I've decided to live my life in a way that is free of second thoughts, grateful for all the situations I've been blessed to be a part of.

Yan Keuwo is a sophomore from Olathe, Kansas. He is a member of the Braves football team. Yan is majoring in exercise science and plans to graduate in 2023. Following graduation, Yan plans to apply to graduate school.

DERRIANE MORRISON

If I had to describe how much I have changed since my first year of college, I would say that I have done a 180-degree flip—not quite the full 360 but still a noticeable change. Now that I have started my second year at Ottawa, I am no longer the same person I was when I first got here. I can honestly say that I am not the same person I was at the beginning of this semester or even a week ago. Even though this is my second year, I was still not sure what to expect. The pandemic has really obstructed my understanding of what being a college athlete was supposed to be like or what it has been like for the people ahead of me (thank you, planet earth).

This year was like a restart button on my college experience, a complete turnaround and a slap in the face as if it meant to goad me into getting my life together and to try again. While I was not walking around aimlessly and attempting to pretend to know where I was going, I was clueless as to what I was coming back to. To start the year off, I was living off-campus and returning to a completely different wrestling team. After our head coach left at the start of the second semester, I was not sure what our team would look like in the future. I could not have been more nervous coming back to Ottawa.

I have also taken note of how college is extremely different than high school. The staff and students are constantly changing, and the people that we have quickly decided to become our friends are not guaranteed to return. This is not a deep observation for someone who likes to keep the number of people they trust small and consistent (I have maybe five friends in total). A lot of the students that I had become close to my freshman year did not come back to Ottawa. This situation in particular is what caused a major change in how I approached the upcoming school year. Everything and almost everyone was entirely new to me. My goal for this year was to try to stay positive and keep an open mind. Little did I know that this year required more than just positivity but strength.

My transformation into the person I am today began over the summer. I realized that there were a lot of odds stacked up against me, like *a lot*. Just in case anyone is interested in said odds, here they are:

1. My best friend did not plan on coming back to Ottawa.
2. The other friends that I had made also decided not to return.
3. I had just gotten shoulder surgery from a dislocation that took place three months earlier.
4. The wrestling team had just hired a first-year coach.

What else could go wrong?

I had no clue as to what I was coming back to considering I believed I had lost a lot of what was most important to me. To be completely honest, I had thought about transferring somewhere else but something about Ottawa kept drawing me back. I had a lot of time to think about what I wanted for myself. I decided that I needed to continue my education, try to wrestle again, and give Ottawa another chance. Also, I have proven myself to always see things through, good or bad (a pro and con characteristic). So, before moving in, I concluded that all of the reasons I had to leave were just as good enough reasons to stay. I spent the entire summer focusing on my rehab and mentally preparing myself for the upcoming semester.

Once the second semester finally began, I had no idea what was in store for me. No amount of summer preparation readied me for what was unfolding before my eyes. My life seemed to have taken a page out of a screenwriter's college drama series. Every weekend released a new episode where I was completely unaware of the plot. I had not realized how much I had matured until the entire story played itself out (Derri 1, Life 0). That experience forced me to grow and take notice of things that I once believed only happened in movies. Thankfully, I did not have to deal with this stress alone. I could not have imagined going through that whirlwind of events with anyone other than my roommate. The issue took care of itself by the end of the semester, but I will never forget how it continues to shape my life.

In regards to my wrestling, I have gotten better. I learned to use this recovery time as a way to reevaluate what the sport means to me. In all of my years of wrestling, I have never understood so much in such a short amount of time. As someone who tends to be quiet, I finally started to find my voice. At the beginning of the season, we wrote a list of goals for ourselves and for the entire team. From experiences I have had in the past, I did not expect most of the team to take them so seriously. When I wrote down that I would like to learn to be more vocal, my coach took that statement to heart. He made it his job to make sure that I have various opportunities to speak out with the team.

Our new head coach put a lot of trust in me despite only knowing me for a few months. From my time on the sidelines, I saw wrestling from a different perspective. By being given the chance to run practices and help coach during tournaments, I formed a new confidence in myself that I did not realize was there. While this was not the ideal situation to learn about these new traits, I made the most out of it. My training was never deferred as I kept getting closer to being cleared. Once I fully understood the importance of my physical health, I began taking better care of my body so I can wrestle for as long as possible.

This past year, I felt like I had to grow and mature faster than I could mentally keep up. Sometimes I wonder how different this journey to my current life would have been if younger me had gotten to see how we turned out. Would I not have let the small things get to me? Or not spend so much time feeling down about myself? Maybe I would have been more patient with the people around me and not as giving to the people who did not deserve me. Every day, I am getting closer to becoming the person I have always dreamed of being.

Dear first-year-self,

Life gets better. You get better. I know that at times things were not looking up for you, but life always has a way of working itself out. If I could go back in time and give you some great advice, it would be never to be afraid of communicating how you feel. I can honestly say that this trait will come in handy and save you from many bad situations with people. Now that we are older I have a better understanding of why you let others treat you the way you did. You put the needs of other individuals before your own and gave more than what they gave you.

Just know that if you cannot open up about how you

feel and be accepted for it, those people were never meant to be in your life in the first place. Remember that we are continuously learning as we get older. The best people learn from their mistakes and we have made plenty and that is okay.

I would also advise you not to be so hard on yourself. Most people do not get things right on the first try, so cut yourself some slack. You're too young to be stressed out about things that are out of your control. The best way to solve any problem is by living in the moment. We have to remind ourselves of this to this very day. Life will pass you by if you are always set on overthinking about what the future holds. No matter what happens, you will always be okay. There has never been a situation in your life where things did not come together in the end, so just enjoy the ride.

I can't wait to see what the future holds for us. We can dream pretty big and we do not let anything or anyone get in the way of those dreams (a pro and a con in our list of characteristics). This change is only the beginning. We are learning so much about ourselves and how to navigate the world around us. With exactly two years left of college, I cannot promise you it will be easy. However, I can promise you that it will all be worth it in the end.

Love,

Present me

Derriane Morrison is in her second year from Houston, Texas. She is a member of the Braves women's wrestling team. Derriane is majoring in exercise science and expects to graduate in the fall of 2023. Following graduation, Derriane plans to apply to the KU medical school to pursue physical therapy.

ELI OWINGS

Before I was accepted into Ottawa, I was kind of lethargic. I barely put in more effort than was strictly necessary to complete any school assignment or task put in front of me. That's not even considering my demeanor in class, for I was possibly the quietest kid the teachers had seen in a while. Yet still, this lackadaisical attitude and doing the bare minimum, were enough to cruise through the entirety of high school, which didn't give me any incentive to change my mindset. Heck, I didn't even study for any, and I mean *any*, test we had in those four years, and I still only got below an eighty percent once in my memory.

The first piece of advice I'd give myself in my freshman year at Ottawa is this: Take this seriously. I was so used to riding on the easy waves, rising to the next setting was a difficult adjustment, but I didn't change how I did anything in regards to my academics. Even in my social life, I didn't put myself out there to make any friends. I was content to go to class, take my notes, get out, go home, go to work, and relax. Since I didn't put any extra effort outside of class, the material was keen on slipping away from me when I needed it because my brain wasn't used to retaining anything more than the most basic of information that was put into my memory. These bad habits culminated in my chemistry midterm exam of this year, on which needless to say, I flopped. I had never done that bad on anything academic before, which helped the message finally sink in that I couldn't just rest on my laurels and cruise through like I did in high school.

I've been trying to put more effort into studying after class and work, but it's been difficult. After all, bad study habits are difficult to break. I like to think I've made progress. I'm certainly more confident about my finals for all of my classes with this renewed drive. I definitely think I'm better at retaining the information now with these adjustments to my studying routine. We'll see how these adjustments helped me, however, after I find out how I actually did on the finals.

I also have someone I can safely call a close friend, though his name will go unmentioned here. Though he's proven to be an all-around upstanding guy. I hope we'll continue to keep in contact through the rest of our time here and when we pursue our own careers. I'm definitely going to try and find more close friends like him, hopefully even a partner.

There are still many habits that hinder my growth, I'm certain, but I do not know them off the top of my head. However, when I can identify them, and how exactly they're holding me back, I can begin the process of breaking those bad habits too.

Again, the advice I'd give to my freshman-year self would be, "Take this seriously. You absolutely cannot just breeze through everything with the same devil-may-care attitude like you did in high school."

Honestly, there are a lot about my academic habits that I need to curb before it results in consequences I can't bounce back from. Actually, I realized this after that flopped midterm exam and as I was writing this. There are ways people change, however small, almost every day. They could begin to doubt something they thought they knew, perhaps they're having a crisis of faith, maybe experiencing a paradigm shift that alters their perception of right and wrong entirely, but following this new way of thinking could burn the bridges that they cherished for so long. I personally began to doubt if I was actually smart enough to have earned my Top Scholar award in the first place. This is definitely *not* the mindset one needs in normal life, let alone for the upcoming end of the fall-semester finals.

I've been assuring myself that this was not the case. The faculty of Ottawa University would not have chosen me for this scholarship if they did not believe I deserved it. I have faith that they have faith that I can succeed, both here and in my chosen career. I need to learn to accept the assurances that I can do something even when I myself do not believe I can and the assurances seem empty. Sometimes, all it takes to change someone is to simply believe that they can.

The help of the faculty simply cannot be understated. When I saw how terribly I did on that exam, I was distraught. When I went to my teacher to speak to him about how someone who (not to toot my own horn) normally does so well in class could have failed so spectacularly, he sat me down and tried to advise me. It was mainly his advice that I've been incorporating into my new study routines after all. He said that few people were ready for the transition from high school to college, and that one failure did not undo all my other accomplishments. He told me to revisit the materials in lecture, and most importantly, do the assigned reading. I knew he didn't mean to simply skim the topics, but to really *read* them and gain an understanding. If I could truly come to understand how x chemical reaction occurred, or how to find y amount of chemical z in this compound, everything else would come naturally.

I cannot yet give any concrete examples demonstrating how these small yet important changes have improved my material retention, but I have faith that they'll make all the difference in the world. People have an unfortunate habit of dismissing the smaller changes to oneself and others because they believe these changes are too small to have any impact at all. Those who do this underestimate just how much a tiny change in the right aspect in a person's way of thinking can cause them to almost do a complete factory reset on certain aspects of how they tackle some problems.

I feel like this cannot be stated enough; change doesn't have to be drastic, world-shattering revelations. They can be as simple as doing something in a specific way that might not be the optimal way to get what you want in the end. In fact, it is my personal belief that it is the smaller changes that matter the most, because those are sometimes more noticeable than the larger ones.

It is similar to my little brother, who was a pest for most of my life. He would annoy me constantly, always with the little things, like entering my room to gently poke me, or simply looking at me with mischief in his eyes. He even pulled the oldest trick in the book: blaming me for the messes he made and getting me into trouble, though this was when we were both much younger. Heck, I'm pretty sure I programmed myself to be annoyed every time he was in the same room as I. When he got his job last year, however, he became more mature, and the smaller things he did that irritated me stopped almost entirely. I am noticeably calmer around him. I didn't bother to hide my annoyance and occasional anger over his antics, which I'm sure he appreciates at some level. I hope our relationship continues to improve, and I genuinely want us to grow closer. I want to be a better big brother.

I have changed in many small ways in a very short amount

of time, mostly attributed to the domino effect of small realizations stemming from a horrible performance on a chemistry midterm exam. How could anyone have thought that would happen? Change comes from unexpected sources, and the root causes for why those changes occurred in the first place are often completely unrelated to anything further down the line, but the core message that began the string of dominoes falling remains the same throughout every subsequent one.

Almost every single one of my changes was tiny and seemingly insignificant. If someone would have told me about these changes without having gone through them myself, I would have outright laughed in their faces. Yet, having actually gone through this string of revelations, I thoroughly underestimated how powerful the small, insignificant changes can be to a person's mentality, and even their overall demeanor.

I hope to continue to develop into a good and more complete person as I continue my tenure at Ottawa University, and especially beyond my Ottawa years when I'm pursuing my chosen career path. I know whatever kind of person I grow into, Ottawa will do its best to ensure it is one I can be proud of. I was nervous and unsure, even with the full ride offered, to attend, because I didn't think it would offer anything different from my high school days. I am more than happy to say that I have been proven soundly wrong.

Eli Owings is a sophomore from Kansas. He is not a member of any extracurricular activities, but plans to change that in the coming year. Eli is majoring in biology and expects to graduate in 2024. Following graduation, he plans to pursue a career as a physician's assistant.

SECTION THREE

Having completed more than half of their college education, third-year scholars are asked the following question, "What, in your opinion, is the real purpose of a liberal arts education? What are you most excited for about your future?"

People often tout the benefits of a liberal arts education. Further questioning, however, often reveals that these same people don't have a firm grasp on what such an education consists of, or what special features render a liberal arts education particularly valuable—and why.

Our third-year scholars, on the other hand, are in the trenches, fighting to successful navigate that liberal arts education. It is instructive to hear from them as to what they value about their education, and to hear what they are planning to do with the investment they have made. I'm glad to say our students have planned well, understand the value of their education, and are prepared to make the most of the opportunities coming their way. I'm sure you'll agree.

KAYLEN ASHLEY

A liberal arts education, in the words of the college of humanities and social sciences at the University of Northern Colorado "makes people happier and life more enjoyable." While I cannot say that this is true for everyone, I can say that I believe it to be true for myself. In my three years at Ottawa, I've taken many courses, ranging from Quantitative Methods in Business to Basic Issues in Philosophy. Trying to fill my eight breadth areas has taken me all over the map, but after all the hours spent wondering "why am I taking this class? I'm a business major," and "Why do I need to write a paper? I'm a business major," as well as the occasional study sessions ending in tears, I do believe I emerged as both a better student and person. To explain what I believe the purpose of a liberal arts education to be, I will explain first what a liberal arts education means, followed by what I learned outside the normal curriculum from several of the classes I've taken, and ending with what I look forward to after finishing my liberal arts education.

Before I get into my personal opinion on liberal arts education, I am going to briefly talk about someone else's opinion on liberal arts education. Every description of a liberal arts education I could find on the internet shared the same characteristics, but here is my favorite one that I read on the Lyon College website:

> "A liberal arts education focuses on an holistic approach: opening the mind to new ideas, pondering concepts all around us, considering perspectives through new lenses, and understanding differences in thought.
>
> A liberal arts education exposes you to the arts, humanities, social sciences, mathematics, and natural sciences. It teaches you how to learn, and how to evaluate arguments and experiences."

Many people assume that "liberal arts" is politically charged and take issue with that, which doesn't quite make any sense to me. How would a biology degree path be politically charged? No one is saying "if you're a Republican, you can't study these plants." I think a majority of those who oppose liberal arts universities have a serious misunderstanding. Liberal arts has nothing to do with politics, unless of course you are a political science major, in which case it definitely has a lot to do with politics. A liberal arts education in its simplest form is a curriculum that takes you outside your major by requiring certain breadth areas to be studied. The eight breadth areas are creative and performing arts, historical and cultural perspectives, social and behavioral sciences, mathematical and logical systems, natural sciences, language and communication, health and wellness, and theological and philosophical perspectives. These areas are part of the holistic approach as mentioned in an earlier quote. They serve to broaden our horizons so to speak.

First, we have Art Appreciation with Professor Fulton-Miller. For starters, I was terrified of this class for two reasons: 1) I thought it was going to be boring; and 2) I know absolutely nothing about art. The most artsy I get is when I color code my planner. However, for breadth area one, most of my other options were classes where I would actually have to make art, and the only thing that scared me more than being bored is having to look at my own creative ineptitude.

The class, thankfully, did not bore me, and I learned more than I expected. On top of knowing more about art history, I gained a different outlook on life than the one from my number and color-coded planner. Where I look at a painting and think "Oh cool, that's some paint on a canvas," a person who is artistically inclined can interpret how the artist felt, how brush strokes make the paint look different to emphasize something important, whether the artist was right or left-handed, if they could juggle or preferred vanilla creamer in their coffee, etc. Where I choose to look at life in objective terms, other people can look at it from a more subjective point of view. None of us are wrong, and I think that's what a liberal arts education is about. People are different, and part of life is realizing and accepting that.

Another class that I never in my life would have expected to enjoy was Basic Issues in Philosophy. Obviously, philosophy classes are going to mess with your head. It's basically the entire point of them; they make you think so hard your brain hurts. However, when you put a group of almost 30 college students of different backgrounds and cultures in the same room and have one man yell strange scenarios at them, it makes you realize just how different people's moral compasses are.

For example, in the trolly problem, where there's a split in the track and one person tied to one side of the track with three tied to the other, I would absolutely pull the lever and run over the one person. I cannot fathom holding the life of one person higher than the life of three other people, unless of course the three people were awful. However, part of what makes this scenario a problem is the lack of information about the people tied to the tracks, which is what stops many people.

Some people also prefer to absolve themselves from guilt by doing nothing, even though this leads to the trolly running over three people. If they had no part of it, then the situation is not their responsibility, as the people would have died anyway. This situation, as with many of the other hypotheticals Dr. Clarke threw at us, required a lot of critical thinking and a clear understanding of our morals. If our minds weren't opened to new ideas by the end of this course, we probably just didn't show up.

Entrepreneurial Economics is one of the required classes from my business economics major, taught by the one and only Dr. Russ McCullough. Any class with Russ is an experience, to say the least, but Entrepreneurial is the one I believe best fits the ideals of a liberal arts education. This class will be the one that makes or breaks you as an econ major. While the other courses focus on the math and graphs, this course is primarily behavioral. If you have ever met me in my life, you know that human behavior makes absolutely no sense to me a majority of the time. I never even have a clue what I am doing, so how should I be expected to understand what other people are doing?

I look at behavioral studies the same way that most people would look at a rabid dog or screaming baby (which is to say I consider them frightening and to be avoided at all costs). A big thing that stuck in my mind from this course is that certain people are just better suited for some situations than other people. It doesn't mean that any one of us is better than the other, just that one person has more of an upper hand in a particular scenario. This is important to a liberal arts education because it's very difficult to understand differences in thought if we never understand that people are fundamentally different.

Technically speaking, this class is not a breadth area course or a course specific to my major, but The Gospels with Rev. Dakota Smith and Dr. John Stanko really did a number on my brain. Coming into college, I was a very outspoken atheist. I had experienced a lot of trauma, both religious and otherwise, and I could not for any reason understand why any all-powerful being would allow it to happen to me. In elementary school, I laid awake every single night praying, and nothing ever seemed to get better. However, throughout the course of this class, I understood why religion was so important to so many people.

I have a very hard time changing my mind about big things like that, so I won't say that it converted me, but it definitely came closer than most. Having an open mind is something I would say is imperative to be a good person, and if you can sit in the auditorium listening to other students talk about how religion has impacted their lives significantly and not at least consider some things, you have bigger issues than college. An open mind and willingness to learn, as well as accept, different ideas is a big portion of what liberal arts education strives for.

What I am most excited for about my future is having all of my hard work pay off for me when I land a nice, cushy desk job making three times as much as I do at the moment. As a full-time student who also works a minimum of 35 hours a week, nothing excites me more than the prospect of a 9:00 a.m. to 5:00 p.m. workday with no other obligations. The idea of having free time to just come home, sit on my couch, and binge watch *Criminal Minds* with my cat, knowing that everything I've put myself through during my college years was worth it, just makes me so ecstatic. I know that seems kind of lackluster, and most of my cohorts are probably going to say something cool and enlightening, but after a life fraught with instability and never being sure of where I would end up, the concept of being so close to having a stable and contented lifestyle brings me a lot of peace.

When I was younger, the only thing I knew about myself was that when I grew up, I wanted to be happy. Obviously, I learned a little bit more about who I am and what makes me happy as I got older, but that one thing remained constant. Everything I've done up until right now, as I sit here typing this essay, has been in the pursuit of happiness for me and those I love, and graduating college is another huge step toward that goal. I love that I am so close to being able to reach my full potential, as well as so close to being able to quit my job at Walmart.

There is nothing wrong with working at Walmart, and I have so much respect for people who are genuinely good at working in customer service. However, I am simply far too irritable and impatient, and I can feel the slow descent into madness and hellfire beginning within me. It is a good job for the time being. I love my coworkers and I earn $16 an hour, but I think if I encounter one more person who tries to explain to me what a pumpkin pie looks like so I can go find one in the back room, I might break down in tears.

As I have said so far in all of my Ottawa Scholar essays, I am so grateful to have been given the opportunity to attend this school. Through OU, I have found my ideal career, some of my best friends, and, most importantly of all, myself. In my time here, I've learned that I'm capable of so much more than I ever realized was possible. During my college experience, I've become 100 percent financially independent and stable, bought a new car, got my own apartment, and kept a 4.0 GPA the entire time. I'm the student president of the Sigma Alpha Alpha Honors Society on campus, which is such a big honor for me.

High school was a rough time for me, so thinking that I had four years left of school used to make me miserable. After finishing two and a half of the years I had left and realizing that I'll be graduating a semester early, I'm almost sad that I have so little time left. College has been a time of astounding personal growth for me, and while I am a tiny bit afraid of it ending, I am very excited to see where it takes me.

Kaylen Ashley is a senior from Oberlin, Kansas. She is the student president of the Sigma Alpha Alpha Honors Society. Kaylen is double majoring in accounting and business economics, and expects to graduate in December 2022. Following graduation, Kaylen plans to pursue financial advising as a career.

BRODY BURKHOLDER

To understand what a liberal education's purpose is, we must first dissect what exactly a "liberal arts education" is. The *Merriam Webster Dictionary* defines a liberal arts education as "college or university studies (such as language, philosophy, literature, abstract science) intended to provide chiefly general knowledge and to develop general intellectual capacities (such as reason and judgment) as opposed to professional or vocational skills." Translated into everyday language, essentially this helps us to understand that a liberal arts education teaches us different languages along with more in-depth English education, philosophy and religion, and different fields of various hard or soft science concentrations in a variety of fields. This is done in order to cultivate "knowledge" and "intellectual capacity" as opposed to "vocational skills" or essentially work done with one's hands or labor that is taught directly by a mentor or on the job. However, in my humble opinion, I have a problem with this definition, due to the fact that it separates the terms/ideas of "intellectual capacities" and "knowledge" from the term "vocational skills." This is a great starting point for the first reason a liberal arts education exists.

Culturally speaking, especially in the last few decades, I believe we have seen a divide in the country much like everyone believes. The country is divided along lines of race, politics, judicial rulings, and almost everything else, including what is perceived as "blue collar" versus "white collar." A trend is emerging amongst today's younger generation in which there is a perceived hate or malice between those who attend college and study academically for four years, and those who attend trade school or perhaps take on a job apprenticeship. Society oftentimes tries to pit these two audiences against one another due to an outdated belief that one is inherently better or harder than the other, which is simply not true. While a liberal arts education doesn't serve to educate anyone with vocational skills, it does not impart the belief that the academic way is better in any way. It simply shows us all the possibilities that exist, and it shows us our lack of knowledge in certain areas.

Now it may seem bizarre or counterintuitive that I am

embracing and not only rejoicing in an education system that exists to show us our weakness in the world. However, I believe it is one of the most important lessons I have ever been taught in my young life. I cannot speak for all academic experiences, nor their upbringing, but in my own personal experience, a liberal arts education has humbled me beyond words. Public school and the typical core-40 curriculum is by no means centralized to one specific subject or specialization. Most students find themselves sticking to or excelling more in areas that they know well, or are naturally talented in. It is not only human nature, but wishful thinking to frequent areas of study that you are already talented in or know more about, as this naturally achieves better grades and an overall better performance.

While there is nothing wrong with this, this typical model of education doesn't incentivize students to break their old patterns of thinking, and it doesn't teach students how to properly learn or "cultivate knowledge." I have said it before in previous essays, and I will say it again: Knowledge based on what one is able to memorize is so vastly different than someone who can critically think or problem solve what lies in front of them. Imagine that if the first time you ever lifted weights, you had a perfectly average bench press, a perfectly average power-lean, but a very high percentile squat. Now imagine if after that initial benchmark, you only ever adjusted weight or trained heavily on your squat and you never took the time to adjust form or weight for any of your other lifts. This is essentially basic public education. A liberal arts education is the personal trainer with a fully stocked and ready-to-go gym for your brain.

The brain functions like other parts of the body. And like any other muscle or any other aspect of the body, it needs to be exercised. It needs to warm up, cool down, rest, and improve like everything else in life. A liberal arts education is the proven formula to put your brain and thought processes through a great workout. By not forcing but exposing me to examine so many vastly different areas of studies along with so many different knowledge sources, I was able to truly gauge where I was in the world and assess my actual intellect, realizing how much room for improvement there was.

I will never forget how humbling my first semester of

college was. I went from being the biggest academic fish in my pond to being the new kid on the block at a new institution with a new way of learning. I was not fully prepared or in the right mindset to learn adequately and at the pace I should have been at until I encountered subject material I knew nothing about. My first ever college "C" was, in hindsight, the best thing that ever happened to me.

This is the beauty of the liberal arts education. It enables us to see ourselves in a different light and allows us to humble ourselves and realize that we all have room for improvement. By studying so many diverse subjects, we gain a vast appreciation for the professors and educators who have given multiple years of their lives to a subject in order to be able to teach it. Additionally, we gain an appreciation for others in the student body who can devote themselves to studying complex and advanced subjects we previously knew nothing about. A liberal arts education additionally forces us to work alongside and coexist with people from all over the country. With so many different and diverse populations, we cannot help but gain untold insight and wisdom from them.

Never before in my life have I been humbled as I have obtaining my liberal arts degree. I have gained much appreciation and insight into new areas of studies and fields that I had previously never even known existed. I believe it is a truly humbling experience to know that you are one small piece of a huge puzzle. It is not a source of weakness not to know everything. It is actually a strength because there is so much room for growth. By learning subjects that are foreign to us, we improve the way our brains categorize information and how we reason with each other and ourselves, along with changing how our brains problem solve. A liberal arts education teaches us not to be individual people, but to be *human*.

I think beyond humbling my own psyche, and illustrating what areas I can grow and improve on, a liberal arts degree has me geared towards the future—a future that while full of uncertainty, is nonetheless exhilarating. It is no secret that the COVID-19 virus has changed the shape and face of the world as we know it, and has probably changed society for the immediate future. Politics and pandemic aside, times have been tough. In instances like this, we must remind ourselves that tough times never last, but tough people do. But what most people are all too quick to forget is that we are in control of our own destinies, and there has never been a tougher generation of individuals to tackle the issues of the future.

As I look ahead to the future, I do so with worry and concern, but also with great joy. I look ahead to the future and share the concerns with every citizen. I worry about the future of our climate and our planet, and I hope it is not too late to change. I worry often about the relations of different races and cultures in the future and hope we can begin to empathize and heal now. I worry much about the future my children will grow up in. However, I have been blessed with spending time and meeting the people who will go on to solve these problems, and this is what brings me great joy.

Americans are correct in the sense that never before have we seen such issues that are now facing the country, and never have we seen such a divide. However, never before have we seen such a talented, capable group of people through which to combat these issues. I had the opportunity my sophomore year to attend the President's Leadership Conference, an annual conference hosted by the Phi Delta Theta fraternity. The event educates members who have been elected on how to become leaders and effectively be presidents of their respective chapters. Typically, the event is hosted annually in St. Louis during which time everyone descends on the city and stays in the same hotel. Overall, it's a very enjoyable spectacle.

However, the pandemic obviously altered those plans as it did everything else. Questions loomed about the event happening at all, and there were concerns about the certainty of our leadership and the fraternity itself. Nevertheless, we pressed on and got the notification we would all be meeting in a Zoom conference room in order to best continue our business as usual. While this itself is not an unusual thing to happen during the pandemic, this was the first time anything on this scale or anything of this importance had ever attempted to be carried out completely online. Never before have I heard such negativity and doubt surrounding an event.

Everyone was upset and angry that such a precious event was being reduced to a Zoom call and the main talk of the town was that people would gain neither actual experience nor any actual value of brotherhood. I would be lying if I said that I had not shared some of these very similar concerns. However, what actually happened, and what I witnessed, was one of the most pleasant surprises I have ever had.

In the face of absolute uncertainty, panic, and fear, people rose to the task. I was part of the largest Zoom call ever in recorded history with a representative from every Phi Delt Chapter across the country and an entire leadership of GHQ, alumni clubs, and CAB chairman to boot. Never before in person or online had I seen such a rock solid group, a showing of people who were all united for one cause. It was so comforting to be in a place and space where everyone has heard and everyone was valued. This is what I see in the future.

We are the generation who has inherited a multitude of problems from climate change, to race relations, to an unscalable mountain of national debt. But what has risen out of these problems is a generation that is equipped and ready to deal with these issues head on. I am continually inspired everyday by my peers and the faculty and students I have met at Ottawa University. The most exciting part about the future is the hurdles we get to overcome together. I am filled with joy and conviction that the odds have never been more stacked against us generationally, but all that means is the victory and triumph will be even sweeter. I am privileged and thankful that I get to share this beautiful life and world with my colleagues and students beside me. I have overwhelming faith that the future ahead is not something to retreat from, but to charge toward. The thing that excites me most about the future is simply that we have one worth fighting for.

Brody Burkholder is junior from Middlebury, Indiana. He is a member of the Phi Delta Theta fraternity on campus, and is majoring in applied psychology. Brody plans to graduate in 2023 and pursue a master's degree in social work.

JESSAMINE GREUTER

In order to comprehend the value of a liberal arts education, one must understand the core principles of such an education. Ottawa University is a liberal arts college. The goal of the University is to help students live a life of significance. A liberal arts education helps to build free thinkers and knowledgeable citizens. A liberal arts education allows students to learn and interact with ideas and people who are different than they are. The idea of a liberal arts education was created in the 1850s with 212 schools being established between 1850 and 1899. Since then there have been over 540 liberal arts colleges established in the United States.

A Liberal Arts Education creates students who are willing to consider options and opportunities outside of their normal realm of thinking. It creates opportunities for students to work with other cultures and backgrounds to create new ideas and understandings. In the classroom, the goal of liberal arts education is to aid students in learning to work with others and to create a mindset of mindfulness about other people's opinions and ideas. This form of education focuses on creating respectful and knowledgeable individuals.

Living a life of significance is accomplished when people touch other people's lives in positive ways. A liberal arts education helps students prepare for such a life of significance. It teaches students how to work with others by taking other people's views and needs into consideration. In the education classes at OU, we often discuss the different types of learners and how to adjust our teaching to the students' individual needs. If a student has ADHD or dyslexia, they will need to be taught differently than another student without those challenges. We learn about proper ways to adjust to the students and their unique ways of learning and comprehending material.

In the future, I look forward to using the skills that I have learned in the classroom at Ottawa in my own classroom. My major is secondary education English and I plan to use this degree to teach middle school language arts. My education at Ottawa University has taught me the importance of being open-minded and considerate of other people. In the future, I plan to have a classroom where every student feels welcome and safe. I plan to accomplish this by having clear rules and expectations in my classroom.

Rule one for my classroom is that you are to respect your fellow classmates, the staff and yourself. Rule two is listen to others and think before you speak. My philosophy is that the classroom should be a place where students feel safe to express themselves and not be afraid of being judged. Learning from other students and new resources is one way students can be positively impacted by the classroom setting. Liberal arts education teaches college students problem-solving skills and new ways to look at problems. It gives students perspective and allows them to learn and grow. I plan to take the tools that I have learned and use them in my future classroom.

I am unsure of where I want to teach in the future. The options and possibilities are endless. Through Ottawa, I have discovered that there is not only one path that I have to follow. I've learned about many different career and life paths that I have the opportunity to take. I could teach in a different country or even simply a different grade level than I had originally planned. When I first started at Ottawa University I thought I knew exactly what I wanted to do. I had planned to teach high school English, I was going to teach in my old high school and I was planning on only teaching English.

Now that I have gone through Ottawa and taken classes in different liberal arts courses, I have discovered a lot about myself and where my interests truly lie. I have discovered that I enjoy history a lot more and plan to pursue a minor in it. I have also discovered many different genres and authors that I had never heard of or had the pleasure of reading. In the future, I plan to incorporate these authors into my teachings and allow students to have a broader access to literature. I have also discovered that I have a passion for writing stories. After graduating, I plan to continue this newly-discovered passion for writing and use it to create books and short stories. Without the classes at Ottawa University, I would never have discovered the many different passions and interests that I hold.

While attending Ottawa, I have had the opportunity to take a large variety of courses. One in particular that I enjoyed the most was Interpersonal Communication. This class allowed me to have a better understanding of how to communicate with others. It also taught us that communication is not always what we think it is. Body language, nonverbal communication, and other forms of communication all work together to allow us to work together. The class taught me that other people do not always communicate the same way I do and that this can be a tool rather than a problem or obstacle. Understanding how others communicate can allow us to build stronger connections and learn things we never would have immediately thought.

I plan to use this in the future when working with students. Some students may not communicate what they are thinking and feeling but this can be understood by looking at how they are behaving in the classroom, how well they work with others, and how they are performing academically. A problem that many teachers have is that they assume a student is failing simply because they are not trying their best, but this is not always the case. We learned in class that there are many factors that go into determining why a student is struggling and we have to be able and willing to look for these signs. This is one example of how every class I have taken at Ottawa University has had an impact on my future and how I plan to perform in my future classroom.

One excellent part of attending a liberal arts college is the opportunity to learn about and experience other cultures. This last semester, the Whole Earth Club hosted a Swedish day in the cafeteria where students were able to try authentic Swedish food and learn interesting facts about Sweden. This occurs almost every semester with different countries each time. At this year's Club, fair students were able to try snacks from France, Sweden, and many different countries. The Whole Earth Club is only one of many ways the students can learn about different cultures and have different cultural experiences. The Whole Earth club has gone on short trips to renaissance festivals, and many different authentic restaurants with cuisine from other countries.

Ottawa University also has had a few other events where students were able to learn about other cultures and lifestyles. On a student life day, Dr. Galiana taught the students about Buddhism and yoga. She not only taught that lecture but a class about this as well. Informative and fun classes such as this one are some of the positive things about attending a liberal arts college. During one of the weekly student life days, students had the opportunity to attend a meeting about the many different travel opportunity experiences going on this year at Ottawa University. These opportunities include a trip to Guatemala, Ghana, and Scotland. The school has hosted many trips in the past including trips to Ireland, Japan, and France.

This year Ottawa University has a liberal arts class called "Tombs and Tales of Ancient Scotland." In this class, students are able to learn about Scottish culture and specifically the Orkney Islands. A main part of the class is that students are required to produce a final project. This project is designed and created by each student who is expected to research and write about something that is of interest to them. The class ends with a trip to the Orkney Islands at the end of the semester. While in Scotland, the students get the opportunity to do hands-on research and finish their projects. I am looking forward to attending this class and trip this coming semester.

Another trip I am looking forward to in the near future is the music department's trip to Chicago this spring. The choir and bands are going to be traveling to Chicago in March to enjoy multiple concerts and museums. It will be an excellent opportunity for the students to learn about different types of music and forms of art. We will have the opportunity to attend a play, view live bands and performances, as well as attend an opera. I am looking forward to learning and enjoying these many aspects of art. This is yet another positive experience that would not be possible without the school's goal of creating an environment where students can learn about the many different cultures and communities in our world.

Jessamine Greuter is a junior from Topeka, Kansas.
She is a member of Ottawa University Chi Alpha.
Jessamine is majoring in secondary education
English and expects to graduate in May of 2023.
Following graduation, Jessamine plans to apply for
a position in the Topeka Public School System to
pursue teaching.

COLLIN HANSON

The idea of a liberal arts education is not exactly a new one. People have been attending universities across the nation with the purpose of obtaining a liberal arts degree for many years now, and while the idea is nothing new, some of the methods of execution are. The fact of the matter is the world is progressing and changing. Things that may have been critically important in the past are relatively obsolete now. Likewise, practices that occur now simply weren't necessary or relevant in the past. This being said, one of the most important ideas to be considered when talking about the purpose of a liberal arts education is the idea of learning to think creatively, innovatively, and diversely through many different pathways of thought.

One of the key goals of a liberal arts education is the ability to think critically. This term has been used often in my time here at Ottawa University, yet it is a term that a lot of people overlook. Critical thinking is essentially the act of looking deeper into various issues and topics by means of asking and answering various questions about the topic, and taking initiative in order to reach certain conclusions. There is a quote by James Baldwin, famous author and activist, that describes the idea of critical thinking well.

> "The paradox of education is precisely this — that as one begins to become conscious one begins to examine the society in which he is being educated. The purpose of education, finally, is to create in a person the ability to look at the world for himself, to make his own decisions, to say to himself this is black or this is white, to decide for himself whether there is a God in heaven or not. To ask questions of the universe, and then learn to live with those questions, is the way he achieves his own identity. But no society is really anxious to have that kind of person around. What societies really, ideally, want is a citizenry which will simply obey the rules of society. If a society succeeds in this, that society is about to perish. The obligation of anyone who thinks of himself as responsible is to examine society and try

to change it and to fight it—at no matter what risk. This is the only hope society has. This is the only way societies change" (Baldwin, James).

Truthfully, critical thinking is the means by which the world progresses, and some people will oppose it, but that does not negate the fact that change can be fantastic. Critical thinking also involves the ability to analyze a situation or issue from multiple perspectives and draw conclusions based on extensive research and findings. The problem is that many people in society are willing to reach conclusions about a subject without properly analyzing it. This is a dangerous practice because it can lead to incorrect conclusions, and can also be divisive if applied to particular situations in which other people disagree.

Furthermore, people who are not willing to look at a situation from multiple perspectives tend to include their own personal biases. I have learned about plenty of diverse and complex topics during my time at Ottawa University, but one of the most important has been the importance of eliminating biases from judgments and research. Bias is a dangerous practice that proper critical thinking can eliminate if done properly. Truly, critical thinking is a goal of the uttermost importance that all universities should strive to teach. Students who learn to critically think are set up for success in almost any career they follow because they are more equipped to solve problems, and they tend to have the capability to get along with other people more easily.

Another important aspect of a liberal arts education is the ability to collaborate with other people of different backgrounds, education, strengths, and weaknesses. The fact of the matter is that not all people have the exact same way of learning and thinking, and certainly not the same opinions. Thus, it is vital that a liberal arts education equips students with the skills necessary to provide efficient and effective collaboration amongst students.

One method of doing this is to offer classes that inform students of the broad ways of thinking philosophically. Many students have different philosophies that impact the way they work with others. When a student understands different philosophies that are not their own, they are more likely to find ways to connect with other students. Religion is another important aspect of so many people's lives and universities must find a way to incorporate this reality.

The truth is, every person must answer the question of whether or not they believe in God. Some people have already answered this question whether they realize it or not, but regardless of what the answer is, it is something that gives different people different purposes and meanings. Therefore, it is vital that universities recognize this and incorporate different activities that include everyone, but also inform everyone about all the different perspectives. It is for this reason that I believe world religions is an important class, and if people don't take the class, then it is the duty of other professors to incorporate the information.

Liberal arts education systems also need to ensure that students are completing activities that require collaboration with other students while not encouraging the dependence on other students. Each person has different strengths and weaknesses, and the best discoveries and inventions require multiple different strengths being utilized. When people work together, they are able to overcome different weaknesses using the strengths of other people. One person may not be very good at communication, but another person can fill in that role. Some problems are simply too advanced and too complex to be solved by one individual. Because of this, it is imperative that we have the ability to work together in order to solve these kinds of problems. Overall, collaboration is a necessary skill that universities must teach and mentor their students in for the purpose of equipping them for success in society.

One of the final aspects of a liberal arts education is the idea of diversity. This world is much bigger than any one person or worldview and the fact is that there are many different types of cultures, backgrounds, ethnicities, and lifestyles of our peers. It is important for a liberal arts university to address as many of these as possible and certainly include all of them. I believe it is important for me to define the idea of inclusion.

The idea of inclusion does not by any means refer to agreeing with every type of decision or lifestyle. For example, as a Christian, I do not believe in the morality of a lot of LGBTQ ideologies. However, it is also my responsibility and role as a Christian to love everyone unconditionally regardless of the decisions they make. After all, I am far from a perfect human being as well, and it would be just as wrong for me to judge another person when I too struggle with morality. It is for this reason that a liberal arts education must teach inclusion to the degree so people learn that disagreement is bound to happen and is not wrong, while respecting and loving other people is crucial.

Another part of diversity is culture. People come from different parts of the world where different cultures prioritize things differently. It is the responsibility of a liberal arts school to incorporate as many activities as reasonable to include these cultures. Truly, there are some traditions within other cultures that people are simply ignorant of because of where they live. However, this does not always have to be the case if a university is doing their part in spreading the ideas of different cultures in the minds of their students. Some cultures even have traditions and ideas that might be a lot of fun for students.

The problem is that often times students are not exposed to different cultures. Exposing students and educating them to different cultures is a positive thing that a liberal arts university should strive to do in order to include more variety and make it more comfortable for people of different cultural backgrounds to thrive. Ethnicity is another important aspect of diversity. Whatever the case may be, all ethnicities are the same in value, but it is important to recognize that not all ethnicities are the same in other aspects such as what they value due to where they come from and how they were raised.

However, it's just as important to recognize that just because someone is from a certain region of the world, or of a certain race, does not mean that they themselves have the values and beliefs that the people associate with that ethnicity. A quote by Chimamanda Ngozi Adichie says,

> "Teach her about difference. Make difference ordinary. Make difference normal. Teach her not to attach value to difference. And the reason for this is not to be fair or to be nice but merely to be human and practical. Because difference is the reality of our world. And by teaching her about difference, you are equipping her to survive in a diverse world. She must know and understand that

people walk different paths in the world and that as long as those paths do no harm to others, they are valid paths that she must respect. Teach her that we do not know—we cannot know—everything about life. Both religion and science have spaces for the things we do not know, and it is enough to make peace with that. All of these things are important for a person to consider and it is imperative that schools be teaching these ideas to students" (Adichie, Chimamanda).

This quote is speaking about females in a time when females did not have the same rights that they do now, but the principle can apply to all diversities. No matter what the age, sex, background, or ethnicity of a person, difference is acceptable and should be encouraged. It is not a bad thing to stand out, and can sometimes even be beneficial. Overall, diversity is an important factor that influences organizations and thus, should be taught in all liberal arts educations.

In conclusion, a liberal arts education can be quite beneficial to a student's life if the university implements it correctly. There are so many important aspects of it that can lead to more knowledge and understanding of many different things. One issue that has not been addressed is that a lot of people receive these educations, but do not know the true purpose of them. If universities were compelled to explain the goal, there might be more willingness and excitement from the students to learn and understand, and the student may even give valuable input. As long as universities themselves understand that the purpose of a liberal arts education is to encourage critical thinking, expand knowledge of existing diversities, and facilitate collaboration, then this type of education will succeed. Finally, it is vital that we as a society understand the role of the liberal arts so that we can implement different strategies to improve the system and create a better environment for the generations to come who may be eager to learn.

Collin Hanson is a junior from Ottawa, Kansas. He is a member of the Braves golf team as well as the president of the OU Disc Golf Club. He is also a leader of FCA and other campus ministries. Collin is a biology major who expects to graduate in the spring of 2023. Collin is unsure of his plans after graduation but wants to apply to the Kansas University Medical School to pursue a career in medicine, but will also be applying to pursue a career in medical device/technology sales.

LAWSON MEDLEN

The beauty of a liberal arts education is based on its core foundation in two categories. The first can be explained as humanities-type courses, which include that of philosophy, literature, and the human mind. The second is the broad business areas and subjects, such as my own subjects: economics, finance, and accounting. I believe that in combining these two different areas of thought, our minds can focus on growing intelligence by applying math and ideology to the desires of others, whilst also pursuing solutions to modern-day issues. This truly leads to a higher level of development and enrichment in society.

How might a liberal arts education be used most efficiently? In my opinion, this education prepares students to solve real-world issues. It not only gives us the tools necessary to succeed in a difficult world, but it also gives us the tools and *sense of mind* of what we can do to better the world. A year ago, I would not have been writing this paper with such large self-intentions in my head. I wanted to be a completely selfless person. I can see now that in order to help the world I must first better myself and become the best possible version of myself.

In pursuing these degrees, I have found that what I'm learning in class is affecting my daily life. I have started looking around at different cities, wondering how a business can succeed and help improve the lives of those around them. I've wondered whether different laws and political ideas will help the people, giving them the tools and freedom they need to succeed. The liberal arts education gives us an education for many real-world jobs, often involving money, people, and numbers. But while giving us a secure job which we enjoy, it also gives us a greater understanding of the world. I myself have had a change in thinking, as I'm constantly wondering how people will react to different economic scenarios. Understanding the people of the world and the world itself will give me a greater awareness of what I believe is right and wrong, securing my ethics and values.

This last semester, I have come to really appreciate my education. It has developed a sense of confidence in my mind. I see now that there are so many ways to impact the world positively, and that a serious effort can make a difference. If I don't like some-thing, there is a respectable way to go and have it changed. If I have a strong argument backed by good reasoning and data, while putting the effort in to change the world, I will be heard by those I go to. I must always have a plan, and try my best to stick to that plan. Sometimes major inconveniences come along the way and shake this plan, but being open to change, and sticking to what I desire and believe, I will succeed.

This education is helping me formulate the plans to help other people and myself. I've found myself more patient around every person I meet. I now understand that they could have com-pletely different opinions than mine due to their subjective rea-soning, and I respect that reasoning. In following this mutual re-spect in others, you too may find yourself more open to new connections that improve your life! All this can come from being more patient, rational, and understanding of the "humanities." At the same time, you may be improving their lives through sharing your own experiences and thought process, adopted from a liberal arts education.

Now we come back to the question, "What is the purpose of a liberal arts education?" In my opinion, a liberal arts education is an education to understand the world, how it runs, and ideas/in-tentions of those living in it. To me, this means that the purpose of a liberal arts education is to prepare students to react to real-world scenarios they may not otherwise have considered.

Students graduating may find themselves confident in what they're doing with a sense of control over their own career and their capabilities. A liberal arts education shows the student their capabilities, while leaving room for them to improve themselves and the lives of those around them as well. It's this awareness of one's capabilities, along with the notion that there is always room for improvement, that allows individuals to prosper in their re-spective fields. Overall, the purpose of a liberal arts education can be found in Ottawa University's motto, "preparing for a life of significance."

I am ecstatic over my future. I want to finish up my bach-elors in business economics and accounting, and possibly go on to graduate school to study business. If given the opportunity, I'd be more than happy to improve Ottawa University in any way possible. Even as a private school in small Ottawa, Kansas, I can see there are lots of ways I could positively change the school after I graduate. I know that after I get out of college, or possibly while still in college these next years of my life, I want to focus on developing a business. I want to produce something for the people. to create a product or service everyone really desires, and give it to them for the cheapest price I can. I'm excited because helping them helps me, and it will help my employees. I find that this is the best way for me to have a positive impact on people's lives, as it's always been my sole goal to help other people. If I really focus on helping them and giving them what they want, I'll help the maximum number of people I possibly can.

Although it may take a while for me to get to where I want to be in life, I'm very excited for everything else to come in the meantime. Seeing the world and experiencing it with friends and family are high priorities. I'd love to see the world and travel to places I'd never even considered in the past. Getting out into the real world while taking fun trips can really put things in perspective. I've lived in Ottawa almost my entire life, and finally getting out to see other areas of the world will help me. I'll see what one place may be doing right or wrong, and how to improve others' lives closer to home.

The chance to make a real-world difference out of college is very exciting. I know that I'm getting the tools I need to make the difference, and I'm eager to use them. Even now, through living in my own apartment, working outside of school, spending time with friends, studying hard, and paying attention in class, I feel I'm destined to do great things. I will take whatever I can as it comes to me, and shrug my shoulders at the worst of it. If I keep my head up high, and focus on working my hardest, giving it my all, and doing the best with what I have, I will be completely fulfilled. Hopefully along the way I can find myself also providing for a family of my own, producing for and influencing their lives in the best possible way. I'm excited for the opportunity to be a great husband and/or father one day, and that will be my top priority. Overall, this goal triumphs most, as family is something I've come to value more and more during my time here at Ottawa. I want to give and improve the lives of my kids, and hopefully pass on to them whatever valuable knowledge I've attained.

I'm also excited to expand my faith in the future. Recently, I have begun digging deeper into my religion. Reading the Bible has become very important to me. My time at Ottawa has influenced my perspective on religion in a positive way. If I ever find myself financially fortunate, I'd want to donate as much as I could to those living in poverty. I mean, take Keanu Reeves for example. He just donated 70% of his earnings from the latest *Matrix* movie to cancer research. This truly is a goal of mine, and I don't intend to forget it. I want to love others as I love myself and treat them always with the best of intentions.

If I had one thing to look forward to in the future, it's going to be my continued growth. I've grown a lot in the past few years of college, completely changing myself. Every step I've taken to be a stronger and more independent person has felt great. I know that no matter how good or bad the future may be, I still want to focus on growing myself. This growing includes learning new skills, reading more books, and giving what you can back to the world.

If given the opportunity, I would want to run in some sort of political campaign. If I could spread the knowledge I've gained to help those in poverty, I would. Seeing lots of hate, I know the two-party system we see today could be drastically changed. The world is becoming a smaller place right now, and I have my own predictions on what is to come economically in the next few decades. We're going to need people with the type of thinking the Gwartney Institute and a liberal arts education gives. We're also going to need people who have mutual respect for one another, someone who can effectively get their point across without insulting other's personal dignity. This is something I believe we're lacking in our society today.

The future is uncertain, and there is no knowing for sure what will happen to me. I've decided life will be fine so long as I follow the morals I have now. I know many things will be changing, and my life will be a roller coaster of easy/hard events. This uncertainty is exciting to me, because I don't know what my full capabilities are in life, since I have yet the chance to reach them. Just as a young adult, I've only begun tapping into my potential. I have found by helping other people, I find my mood, and my life improves. It's a mutual exchange in my mind: helping others and feeling the great satisfaction in doing so. This feeling is liberating, and almost always beats any "bluesy" moods I may have. No matter how hard or easy my life may be, so long as I work hard, love others, and stick true to myself, I will be happy. I know that through owning a business, managing a business, or running for an office will be the best way I can do this.

In summary, what am I excited for in the future? To give the world my mind, my heart, and my greatest effort. No matter how much I succeed or fail, I'm excited to help others and give it my best effort. It's my opinion that a man's best effort is the greatest thing to bring to the world. This is something that we are seeing less and less of due to the luxuries in our modern-day world. Life is easy! And technology is making it easier, but we must remember to run our *own* lives. In doing this, a man is giving his honest best and controlling the life around him. It's through this that people find the next best way to improve others' lives, by improving their own in their own unique way.

Every person is different, and we should value this difference. Controlling your life and having an innovative mind in doing so will make the world, your world, a better place. Bring something to the table, and you will find yourself and those around you happy and prosperous. I'm really excited to see what I can bring to the table, and the chances to do so are only opening up more and more for me through the years. I know that somehow I will make the world a better, happier place to live in.

Lawson Medlen is a junior from Ottawa, Kansas. He is the president of the only campus fraternity, Phi Delta Theta. Lawson is majoring in business economics/accounting, and expects to graduate in the spring of 2023. Following graduation, Lawson will apply for a position as an accountant or financial advisor, while pursuing his entrepreneurial dreams.

SECTION FOUR

Graduating scholars faced a choice. Some scholars chose to answer, "How has Ottawa prepared you for a life of significance?" Other scholars submitted a piece of coursework they were especially proud of. In either case, the results are interesting and illuminating.

These pieces are all well worth your time, and they highlight the work that our Scholars are capable of as they leave our institution, ready to take their skills and knowledge wherever they land. These students have left their mark on Ottawa, and we are excited that they are taking a piece of Ottawa with them, intellectually cross-pollinating their surroundings as they move toward the bright futures which lays ahead of them.

ANGEL GARRETT

HOW HAS OTTAWA PREPARED ME FOR A LIFE OF SIGNIFICANCE?

For the past four years, I've had the pleasure of continuing my education at Ottawa University. Most people would turn away from a small private NAIA school, but Ottawa drew me in the first time I stepped on campus for my visit day. I was immediately attracted to the beautiful campus and the people who just instantly made the college feel like home. Once I did a cheer clinic here and met the team, I knew that this was where I wanted to continue my education.

There is a saying under the school's seal: *Prepare for a Life of Significance.* The way that I interpret this is to prepare for a life of importance that is worthy of attention. In another way, it means to stand out in life, and I think that this college has made that possible for me. Ottawa University has prepared me for a life of significance through the liberal arts education provided here, the relationships it has allowed me to develop, and the lessons and opportunities it has taught and provided for me beyond the classroom.

The first way that Ottawa prepared me for a life of significance is through the liberal arts education all students are provided with on this campus. A liberal arts education encapsulates all major fields, such as humanities, arts, social sciences, and natural sciences. Ottawa University requires all students to complete what it calls breadth areas that fall under one or more of each of the major fields. These classes include psychology of religion, the Gospels, human services, creative writing, college algebra, and many other options available to all students.

Having the opportunity to explore other areas of education has been something that I have enjoyed immensely in my time here, and I believe it has given me a more well-rounded view on life and how the world works. Not only has the liberal arts education provided me with this different outlook, but it has also allowed me to explore every field and determine if the two that I have chosen for my major are the ones I want to continue with. This is something that I have found quite beneficial because it solidified what I wanted to do in the future by giving me the opportunity to lay out all my options. Biology and psychology are two very extensive and intense majors that require a lot of work outside of the classroom as well as inside. With this liberal arts education, Ottawa has also provided me with a break from my major-level classes so that I am not constantly in a cycle of only difficult classes, but able to indulge in subjects that I find interesting outside of my major—such as English and writing.

Another way that Ottawa University has prepared me for a life of significance is through the relationships I have been able to develop in my time here. College is extremely difficult, not just in an educational sense, but in a social and emotional sense as well. The educational process itself is stressful, not to mention that college is the time that individuals start to come into adulthood and figure out how they want to live their lives. College has not been easy for me in this sense.

There has been both a lot of good and a lot of bad in my time at Ottawa University, but mistakes and missed chances are how people learn and surrounding ourselves with the right people can keep us on the right track for the good to outweigh the bad. Relationships and friendships have been a struggle to maintain, but those that have persisted are the ones that have made my experiences here worthwhile. I've made friends here that I can't imagine having gone through college without. College is not only where you find yourself, but it is also the time that you find the kind of people you want to be around in life and that you want to have relationships with for more than just the school year.

As a school that is around 90% athletes, Ottawa has many different teams on campus, each populated with people from all over the world. Although we all come from different backgrounds and even different states, our team is the first layer of friendship that we create as freshmen here. Not only do we spend most of our time with our teammates, but we are the only people who truly understand what we are going through with our sport or activity. Only other athletes and teammates will understand the stress of balancing practice, weights, and games.

For me, my cheer team was the start of my relationships at Ottawa. I was always a quiet person, but my team helped me to branch out and make friends outside of them, but still stay close to the ones I would be around most often. Along with our team, we get close to people who are in our same major. I've noticed this especially in the Applied Psychology major here on campus.

In this major, we do many group activities that allow us to have fun with each other and grow closer as individuals. Many of my friends here are within my two majors, as we understand the struggles of classes that others in other majors will not understand looking into our major. Those friends are the ones that I have been able to study with while trying to make sense of confusing lectures.

Ottawa also has a wide variety of different clubs and groups that are available to students of any age or background. These clubs include Fellowship of Christian Athletes (FCA), Black Student Union (BSU), biology club, student senate, as well as many others. I've made so many friendships here that will last a lifetime because of all the opportunities to get involved, and these friendships have and will continue to last, despite state lines and time differences.

Not only have I been able to make lasting friendships here, but in a small school like Ottawa, I was also able to develop strong relationships with my professors. The professors here care about the success of their students and take the time to get to know them, especially the students who care about what happens throughout their education. The professor that I have grown closest with here is Dr. Pilar Galiana-Abal. She has been an incredible influence in the classroom, as well as one outside of it. She cares about the mental well-being of her students and is always willing to have conversations with them about whatever is on their mind. I always know that if I'm having a bad day, her office is a place I can go to talk, and I always leave feeling better after speaking with her than when I first sat down in front of her desk.

She has also given me many opportunities to explore different areas of psychology that aren't in the curriculum for an undergraduate. As an applied psychology major, all students are required to write a 30-to-45-page senior thesis on a topic relevant to their course of study in the degree program (either criminal or cultural psychology). Dr. Pilar Galiana-Abal has been an incredible help in the creation of my senior thesis and has continued to be an ever-present aide in this lengthy project. Not only that, but she has recently developed a master's degree in applied psychology that many of her students are extremely excited to take part in. She has been a great influence and one of the main driving forces to push me to go to new heights in my education and to explore areas of my thoughts I never thought would be possible.

I also grew very close to Dr. Thomas Wiese in my years at this university. He has been a great help in defining what I truly want to do and the science behind how I need to get there for my future career. Not only has he helped me with my future, but he has helped me through understanding difficult subjects in biology and other life situations as well. Biology majors tend to be very stressed because of how much work it takes to actually graduate with a bachelor's degree in the major.

All biology majors must complete an oral and written exam for the program, as well as a senior research project of their choice. Dr. Wiese has been an incredible help with the development and execution of my senior research project, and I know that he will be a huge help with my other senior level projects in the months that remain of my undergraduate degree here. Both of these professors have been there for me when I needed their help and will always be people that I respect and appreciate. Without the relationships that I have made here at Ottawa University, I think it would have been much more difficult for me to go through college.

The third way that Ottawa University has prepared me for a life of significance is through the lessons that I have learned beyond the classroom. This school has created so many opportunities for me in life that I never thought I would have the chance to experience. One of these opportunities was to compete with my team three times at college cheerleading nationals in Daytona Beach, Florida. This is an experience most cheerleaders only dream about, but I have been able to live it multiple times.

Not only is the road to nationals an extremely long and difficult one, it is also emotionally taxing as well. Staying late over winter break for extra practices, then coming back early for even more practice, are hard both on the body and the mind. We want to give up and just make it all stop, and sometimes we even start to dread being around our team because of how much time we spend together. In the end, however, it's all worth it to get that feeling of performing on the Bandshell. This experience has been an amazing lesson every year because of how much it has taught me the need to persist through the hard patches of life, even when

I really want to quit. It has also taught me the value of surrounding myself with people who share a common goal, because reaching that goal with friends, practically family, is better than anything.

Another opportunity that has been provided to me through Ottawa University was my internship through the Kansas Bureau of Investigation (KBI) this past summer. I was able to take part in a project with the biology department at the KBI for three months that helped me to understand what forensic science is really like and how casework is conducted in the criminal justice system. I got not only to observe DNA analysis of evidence, but also to witness court testimonies and training protocols that are part of the Federal Bureau of Investigation (FBI) protocols. My whole goal for my future has been to work for the FBI after college, and this experience at the KBI put me on an even more firm track to make that dream come true. With this opportunity being provided to me through connections at Ottawa, more opportunities may present themselves in the future due to my experience.

I cannot wait to finish my time here to earn my under-graduate degree at Ottawa University, but I am even more ex-cited to start my graduate degree here. As I stated previously, Dr. Pilar Galiana-Abal has created a new master's degree in Applied Psychology. This new program is set to launch in the fall of 2022 and will allow me to continue my education at the school I fell in love with four years ago. Not only will I be able to continue my education, but I will be able to continue to prepare myself for a life of significance through my continuation here at Ottawa University.

Angel Garrett is a senior from Eudora, Kansas. She is a member of the Braves competitive cheer team and is majoring in biology and applied criminal psychology. Angel expects to graduate in the spring of 2022. Following graduation, Angel plans to continue her education at Ottawa University by enrolling in the applied criminal psychology master's degree program.

BRYNDEN GROW

"THE LIFE OF A STORM"

Our motto at Ottawa is to "prepare for a life of significance." In many ways, I believe I have accomplished that while preparing for my last semester here in the place I now call home. Never would I have thought that this was the road I was going to take when I was a senior in high school, and these past three and a half years of my life have really flown by. I have made lifelong friends, had an abundance of knowledge etched into my brain, and been presented with opportunities that I will cherish forever. I would also like to take this opportunity to thank my major advisor, professor and friend Dr. Ryan Louis, for so much help throughout my career here at Ottawa. He provided me with the knowledge and resources to complete this project that I will be presenting in this paper. I would also like to thank Dr. Justin Clarke for being such a great leader of the Scholars program along with the continuation of opportunities presented to me and other scholars throughout the years. None of this would have been possible without him, and for that, I am forever grateful.

For my final edition to this wonderful publishing opportunity presented to the Top Scholars of Ottawa University, I want to present and talk about something that I have been working on the past year and will continue to work on into my last semester at Ottawa. I am a communications major with a focus in speech. In my speech labs, I have been mixing different parts of weather and life together. There are many different ways weather has been interpreted as life lessons. One we liked to use in football was "the calm before the storm," because we were trained to stay calm and focused before a game so that we could perform the best of our abilities.

There are many different sayings like this, relating to life. What I am presenting to you today is what we call an interpretive speech in the communications world. In this one, I focused on poetry that used weather and storms to talk about life. I still have some tweaks to make to it but it's for the most part completed. I will also be performing this at speech and debate nationals in

Orlando in the spring of 2022. So, without further ado, I present to you my interpretive speech, "The Life of a Storm."

When the storm hits you run for shelter
that's why you are here in my arms
because somewhere behind your eyelids it is raining
the flood is overflowing one drop at a time
down your rounded cheek and onto your chin
it burns like boiling water all the way down
but you don't wipe it away. I do.

Storms have often been used as a metaphor for life, relationships, and personal beliefs. For myself, I have used storms to talk about beauty and power. This performance will showcase the different ways people use storms in poems to relate to life. As you're reading, look deep within yourself and think about how storms can relate to yourself. Today, I will be presenting a series of poems and short stories titled: Permanent Rain by Tallie, Place of Safety by Earley, Inappropriate Behavior by Huscher, Easy Weather by Johnson, In the Storm by Oliver, The Revolution was Postponed because of Rain by Allen. This is a poetic program titled: "The Life of a Storm."

The light went out.
A ghost floated down the street and turned into a lion.
The lion jumped on the roof of the house and roared and clawed
at the shingles and shattered the windows. It picked up the house
and looked underneath it and sucked in a breath and roared
so loudly that she felt her hair lifting away from her head. She
saw daylight. Mud and leaves and grass. She thought Put it back
down and covered her head with her arms.

On Gypsy Hill
I learn to admire
the texture of a cloudy sky,
I watch a rainbow
arch its' back
across Brixton
An island woman

prepares a feast
of curry and callaloo
hoping to lure the sun back,
to help her survive another
day hour minute
but the rain is permanent,
she turns every raindrop
into a stick, her umbrella
becomes a steel drum
and when she dances down the street
in the pouring rain
some whisper
"She's a little loopy yeah?"
but others know
She is missing home.

I could've married you.
We might've been something special.
Two-point five kids.
The mansion, the his, the hers Lexus.
My daddy said you threaded sunlight for me
and not a day didn't go by when your name was mentioned.
Mama said you were perfect on paper,
but I lived my life in four dimensions.
Still it broke me to break you
but I had to let you go.
You were born to exist in places
where beautiful days always unfold.
You wanted to grant me perfect lifelines,
adorn me with seepy, attentive forevers,
fly me south like a bird for winters
but I didn't want easy weather.
I want monsoons,
torrential downpourings of the unexpected,
tornadoes that tear through my terrain
leaving nothing sacred unneglected.
I want unfiltered summer suns
that scorch my skin with the graffiti of light,
hurricanes that rip weathered veins

from beneath the skins of time that want to bleed free.
Without your FEMA, without your cure,
to stand in the midst of the typhoon
with no fear of being spewed.
I want to be chewed up and spit out by sub-zero winds.
Use my wildfire ashes like moths did
to help us build again.
I like my sky broken,
my brazen falling angels of light,
thunder to ring so loud in my ears that I can't swallow,
mudslides that devastate the landscape of my devotion
and droughts that leave my soul hollow.
I want sandstorms that leave pyramids in my lungs,
blizzards of cold, hard words said in the heat of passion,
avalanches we can't take back in tears, with no traction.
I like my clouds shaped like diamonds,
cumulous raindrops with ugly stories to tell.
I want brimstone and hell, winds with no direction,
the aftermath of storms in which
silence is the only sedative.
I want weather that strips me bare,
leaving me nothing to wear
but the innocence I wore as a girl,
and then to be set free like Noah's dove,
carrying the weight of an empty world.
I want floodwaters that never really recede,
and failing light to usher in the evening,
and to lie beneath cobwebs of bare branches
of winter and listen to the universe breathing.
I want the gamut.
And you, you want easy weather,
skies that never ache,
accurate prediction and days that never break.
You want simple ordinary seasons that always align,
but for me perfection is erosion.
I would've crumbled over time if I had married you.
You would've been something special.
I'd have worn the summer solstice upon my finger
and always had the best of better.

You'd have granted me perfect lifelines,
and adorned me with seepy, attentive forevers.
But I want things the forecast could not predict.
I don't want your easy weather.

Some black ducks were shrugged up on the shore.
It was snowing hard, from the east, and the sea was in disorder.

Then some sanderlings, five inches long with beaks like wire,
flew in, snowflakes in their backs, and settled in a row behind the
ducks -- whose backs were also covered with snow -- so close,
they were all but touching, they were all but under the roof of
the ducks' tails, so the wind, pretty much, blew over them.

They stayed that way, motionless, for maybe an hour, then the
sanderlings, each a handful of feathers, shifted, and were blown
away out over the water which was still raging. But, somehow,
they came back, and again the ducks like a feathered hedge, let
them crouch there and live.

If someone you didn't know told you this, as I am telling you
this, would you believe it?

Belief isn't always easy.

But this much I have learned – if not enough else – to live with
my eyes open.

I know what everyone wants is a miracle.

This wasn't a miracle.

Unless of course, kindness – as now and again some rare person
has suggested – is a miracle.

As surely it is.

In the winter we were all depressed
so we leaned our guns against the sofas

and listened instead to Tim Tim Tiree
singing about his dysfunctions:
Sometimes I wonder if ah'll ever be free
Free of the sins of my brutish daddee
Like the cheating, the stealing, the drinking, and the beating…

The weatherman said the 17th would be sunshine and it
wouldn't be too hot--
Tim Tim Tiree doesn't like sweatin'
but that night the weatherman came on crying
saying he didn't control the weather
that God was real
that he's lucky He, God, didn't strike him, the weatherman for
taking the credit sometimes and that he, the weatherman, was in
no way responsible
for the hurricane coming
and that we, the viewers, should
pray Jesus into our hearts
before it was too late

Now we wait for the rain to stop
All forces on the alert
some in Brooklyn basements
Packed in between booming speakers
Listening to Shabba Ranks and Arrested Development boggling
and doing the east coast stomp
Gargling with Bacardi and Brown Cow
breaking that monotony with slow movements--
slow, hip-grinding movements
with the men breathing in the women's ears to
Earth Wind & Fire's Reasons
And wondering what the weather will be like
next weekend.

I really do hope that you enjoyed reading this interpretive piece. While searching books upon books for this piece, it really showed me the extent to which poetry in general isn't known to the world. There are so many poems that I was exposed to that had nothing to do with what I was looking for, but I was delighted to read them anyway. They had a way of enticing me into reading them again and again. This is just one of many ways Ottawa has led me toward a life of significance.

This has also allowed me to travel and showcase the work I've put a lot of time into. This isn't the only opportunity Ottawa has to offer for travel either. One of my courses, called the "Tombs and Tales of Scotland," has a trip planned to the Orkney Islands of Scotland for the summer of 2022. The Top Scholars program provided me with a travel grant to be able to be a part of this and I couldn't be more grateful for this once-in-a-lifetime opportunity to see a completely new part of the world.

The liberal arts studies provided at Ottawa continue to give me knowledge I wouldn't have known at a school that just provides the basic courses needed to get your degree. One of my favorites that has stood out to me was The Great Plains course that dives deep into the great plains area of the United States and southern Canada. Since I'm from Kansas, there were still a lot of unknowns to me about the beautiful place that I've lived in my whole life. Learning about the wildlife, the hidden treasures, and the different cultures and weather events that take place opened my eyes to some many different things that are in the place I call home.

One of the recent courses that I really enjoyed was one taught by Dr. Justin Clarke, called Political Philosophy. In this course, we jumped into the book, *You and the State* by Jan Narveson. This book explores the different kinds of governments and states, from having no government to having total government control. The philosophies of each were very interesting to dive into and it really opened my eyes to different possibilities of government. This course made me critically think in other ways I had not before, and it helped work in a different mindset than other classes had before.

These are just some of the courses and pieces I've had the pleasure of working with during my time here at Ottawa. And while I am sad to see my time here come to an end. I'm sure I will always be enticed to Ottawa in some sort of way, and I couldn't be more excited to see what the future holds for me.

Brynden Grow is a senior from Hutchinson, Kansas. He is a member of the Braves bowling team and the speech and debate team. Brynden is majoring in communications with a focus in speech and expects to graduate in the Spring of 2022. Following graduation, Brynden plans to pursue a job in the communications field.

CONCLUSION

I'd like to thank our scholars and their families. Editing this book has been a pleasure and a blessing. With each volume, I find myself getting to know the students better while also for the first time getting to know scholars who I haven't had the pleasure of directly instructing. These young adults are impressive, their ambition is humbling, and their optimism is inspiring. They are a credit to this institution, their parents, and themselves. I am thankful and excited to spend more time with our returning scholars in the next year, and I wish the graduating scholars the best of luck.

– Dr. Justin Clarke

Made in the USA
Coppell, TX
17 November 2023